Table of Contents

Introduction

Are you tired of the struggle of setting up an outdoor charcoal grill every time you want to enjoy some BBQ? Well, if you want to have nicely grilled food at home, now you can do it all with the help of your Ninja Foodi XL grill. This multipurpose advanced cooking appliance will help you cook a variety of meals in a variety of styles. And if you are new to the whole concept of cooking in the Ninja foodi XL grill, then this cookbook will definitely help you in understanding the basics about the ninja foodi grill and how to cook low carb delicious ketogenic meal. There are more than 70 recipes in this cookbook that will help you cook ketogenic meals in your multifunctional indoor Ninja Foodi XL grill.

About the Ketogenic Diet

If you look at the statistics and the recent rise of chronic diseases in the modern-day society, you will see that how poor dietary habits and sedentary lifestyle is affecting our health. The ratio of obesity, diabetes, heart diseases and high blood pressure has increased considerably over time. The Ketogenic diet has emerged as a perfect dietary formula to counter these health problems, especially obesity; the diet works through a naturally occurring process in the body, called ketosis.

The idea of the ketogenic diet emerged in the 1920s. When doctors treating the patients with epilepsy and other neurological disorders sought dietary changes in the patient's routine to improve mental health condition over time, they discovered that having a low carb diet with no sugar, and lesser carbs and a high amount of fat can not only improve your mental health, but it also improves your physical health, while making you active and allowing you to lose weight.

Ketosis is a natural metabolic process. In the absence of carbohydrates, the body switches to fats in order to release energy. For ketosis to occur, the glucose levels in the blood must be sufficiently low. And in order to keep the glucose reserves, minimal we need a diet that has carbohydrates lower than 50 grams a day and to maintain this restriction on the carb intake. The ketogenic diet restricts the intake of all forms of sugars, starchy vegetables, other high carb products like beverages, baked goods, grains, legumes, fruits, etc.; instead of high carb diet, the ketogenic approach suggests the use of high fat, moderate protein and low carb diet, according to this formula. There are many ingredients that a person on a ketogenic diet can consume. The low carb ketogenic ingredients mainly include meat, seafood, poultry, ads and low carb ketogenic sweeteners, plant-based milk, like almond milk or coconut milk and all the low carb, vegetables and fruit, Seeds and nuts also make a very important part of a low carb ketogenic diet.

Ninja Foodi XL Grill

The Ninja foodi smart XL grill has no parallel when it comes to versatility. The Ninja foodi smart XL grill comes with a base unit with a hood and a front control panel. This control panel have one-touch keys to control all the functions and the manual settings. The keys for cooking modes are given at the bottom of the control panel; above these keys; you can see an LED display that shows the cooking temperature and time. On both sides of the display, there are keys to increase or decrease that time and temperature. There are a different set of accessories that comes with the Ninja foodi XL grill. And you can use any of these accessories to cook according to the recipe. The grill pan is used for grilling all type of food. Then there are baskets to air crisp, the food and suitable baking pans and baking sheets to cook the food on baking mode. This indoor grill comes with six cooking functions, including:

- Dehydrate
- Broil
- Bake
- Grill
- Roast
- Air Crisp

This device allows you to cook on the preset function, as well as on the manual settings. By pressing the manual setting key, the user can easily adjust the temperature and cooking time of the selected mode. On the preset setting, each function shows its own cooking time and temperature, which the user can use according to the type of food.

The Ninja foodi smart XL grill comes with a temperature probe as well. There is a small space given on one side of this grill to keep the probe. The probe can be plugged easily into the ninja foodi grill. This probe can be inserted in meat and any desired meal to probe the temperature during grilling. This feature allows the user to keep track of the internal temperature of the food and get the juiciest and the most tender meat grains after cooking.

So, what are you waiting for? It's about time that you set up this countertop kitchen appliance and start grilling now!

Breakfast Recipes

Grilled Sausages

Prep Time: 10 minutes.

Cook Time: 10 minutes.

Serves: 4

Ingredients:

- 1 lb. sweet peppers, seeded and cut into eighths
- 2 large yellow onions, peeled and cut into coins
- 3 to 4 tablespoons olive oil
- ¼ teaspoon salt
- 2 lbs. sweet sausages

Preparation:

1. Place the sausages, onions and peppers in the Ninja Foodi Smart XL grill.
2. Cover the Ninja Foodi Grill's hood and select the Manual settings.
3. Set the temperature to 350 degrees F and hit the Grill mode.
4. Grill the sausages for 5 minutes per side, onions for 2 minutes per side and peppers for 4 minutes per side.
5. Serve with sausages with veggies and drizzle oil and salt on top.

Serving Suggestion: Serve the sausages with keto bread and fried eggs.

Variation Tip: Add some black pepper for more taste.

Nutritional Information Per Serving:

Calories 312 | Fat 25g |Sodium 132mg | Carbs 4g | Fiber 3.9g | Sugar 3g | Protein 18.9g

Grilled Eggs with Prosciutto and Parmesan

Prep Time: 15 minutes.

Cook Time: 19 minutes.

Serves: 8

Ingredients:

- 4 thin slices prosciutto
- 4 tablespoons butter
- 8 large eggs
- 1/4 cup heavy whipping cream
- 4 ounces Parmigiano-Reggiano cheese, grated

Preparation:

1. Place the prosciutto slices in the Ninja Foodi Smart XL grill.

2. Set the temperature to 350 degrees F and cook on the "Grill" Mode.

3. Cover the grill's hood and grill for 1-2 minutes per side.

4. Layer small ramekins with grilled prosciutto.

5. Crack one egg in each ramekin and top them with cheese.

6. Place half of the ramekins in the Ninja Foodi XL Grill.

7. Cover and cook on Bake mode at 350 degrees for 10-15 minutes.

8. Cook more of the ramekins in the same way.

9. Serve warm.

Serving Suggestion: Serve these cups with keto bread.

Variation Tip: Add sautéed ground chicken or pork on top of eggs.

Nutritional Information Per Serving:

Calories 297 | Fat 15g |Sodium 548mg | Carbs 5g | Fiber 4g | Sugar 1g | Protein 19g

Grilled Ham

Prep Time: 15 minutes.

Cook Time: 3 hours.

Serves: 8

Ingredients:

- ½ cup choc zero maple syrup
- ¼ cup yellow mustard
- 9 lbs. fully-cooked, bone-in ham, cut in pieces

Preparation:

1. Mix mustard with maple and brush over the ham.
2. Place the ham in the Ninja Foodi Smart XL grill.
3. Cover the Ninja Foodi Grill's hood.
4. Select the Manual Mode, set the temperature to 350 degrees F and cook on the "Grill Mode" for 3 hours.
5. Keep flipping the ham after every 15 minutes.
6. Slice and serve warm.

Serving Suggestion: Serve the ham with crumbled crispy bacon on top and fried eggs on the side

Variation Tip: Soak the ham in salt brine to cure overnight, then grill for juicer texture.

Nutritional Information Per Serving:

Calories 134 | Fat 4.7g |Sodium 1mg | Carbs 4.1g | Fiber 7g | Sugar 3.3g | Protein 26g

Grilled Fried Eggs

Prep Time: 15 minutes.

Cook Time: 5 minutes.

Serves: 2

Ingredients:

- 2 eggs
- Black Pepper, to taste
- Aluminum foil

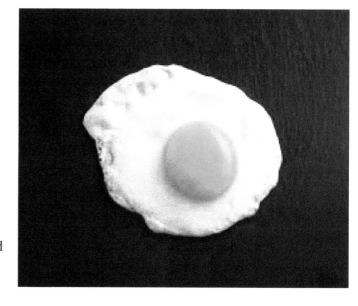

Preparation:

1. Cut the aluminum foil into two small rounds and fold the edges to make a rimmed cup.
2. Crack one egg in each aluminum cup and place them on the Ninja Foodi XL grill.
3. Cover the Ninja Foodi Grill's hood and select the Manual settings.
4. Set the temperature to 350 degrees F and cook on the "Bake" Mode for 5 minutes.
5. Drizzle black pepper on top.
6. Serve warm.

Serving Suggestion: Serve the eggs with bacon and keto bread.

Variation Tip: Drizzle red pepper flakes on top for a tangier taste.

Nutritional Information Per Serving:

Calories 217 | Fat 13g |Sodium 114mg | Carbs 3.1g | Fiber 1g | Sugar 10g | Protein 21g

Grilled Breakfast Sausage

Prep Time: 15 minutes.

Cook Time: 12 minutes.

Serves: 4

Ingredients:

Sausage

- 2 lbs. trimmed boneless pork butt, diced
- 1/2 lb. fat back, diced
- 2 teaspoons salt, to taste
- 1 1/2 teaspoon black pepper, to taste
- 2 teaspoons fresh sage leaves, chopped
- 2 teaspoons fresh thyme leaves, chopped
- 1/2 teaspoon fresh rosemary leaves, chopped
- 1 tablespoon erythritol
- 1/2 teaspoon nutmeg, grated
- 1/2 teaspoon cayenne pepper
- 1/2 teaspoon red pepper flakes

Preparation:

1. Grind pork butter with spices and fat in a food processor.
2. Make 4-6 small sausages patties out of this mixture.
3. Place the patties in the Ninja Foodi Smart XL grill.
4. Cover the Ninja Foodi Grill's hood and select the Manual settings.
5. Set the temperature to 350 degrees F and cook on the "Grill" mode.
6. Grill the patties for 5-6 minutes per side until golden brown.
7. Serve warm.

Serving Suggestion: Serve the sausages with fried eggs and keto bread.

Variation Tip: Add chopped parsley to the patty mixture.

Nutritional Information Per Serving:

Calories 311 | Fat 12.5g |Sodium 595mg | Carbs 3g | Fiber 12g | Sugar 12g | Protein 17g

Cheesy Eggs

Prep Time: 10 minutes.

Cook Time: 10 minutes.

Serves: 6

Ingredients:

- 6 eggs
- ½ cup cheddar cheese, shredded
- ½ cup red pepper, julienned

Preparation:

1. Crack one in the greased cup of a mini muffin tray.
2. Top the eggs with red pepper and cheddar cheese
3. Place the eggs in the Ninja Foodi Smart XL grill.
4. Cover the Ninja Foodi Grill's hood and select the Manual settings.
5. Set the temperature to 350 degrees F and cook on the "Bake" Mode for 10 minutes.
6. Serve warm and fresh.

Serving Suggestion: Serve these eggs with crispy keto bread toasts.

Variation Tip: Add chopped tomatoes to the eggs before baking.

Nutritional Information Per Serving:

Calories 212 | Fat 12g |Sodium 321mg | Carbs 4.6g | Fiber 4g | Sugar 8g | Protein 17g

Bacon on The Grill

Prep Time: 15 minutes.

Cook Time: 14 minutes.

Serves: 2

Ingredients:

- 1 lb. lean thick-cut bacon

Preparation:

1. Place the bacon in the Ninja Foodi Smart XL grill.
2. Cover the Ninja Foodi Grill's hood, select the Manual Mode, set the temperature to 350 degrees F and let them grill on the "Grill Mode" for 7 minutes.
3. Flip the bacon and then continue grilling for another 7 minutes.
4. Serve warm.

Serving Suggestion: Serve the crispy bacon with keto muffins on the side.

Variation Tip: Add some garlic salt or Sugar-free BBQ sauce to season the bacon.

Nutritional Information Per Serving:

Calories 284 | Fat 7.9g |Sodium 704mg | Carbs 6g | Fiber 3.6g | Sugar 6g | Protein 18g

Avocado Eggs

Prep Time: 15 minutes.

Cook Time: 4 minutes.

Serves: 4

Ingredients:

- 2 eggs
- 1 ripe avocado
- Salt and black pepper, to taste

Preparation:

1. Cut the avocado in half.
2. Place the avocados in the Ninja Foodi Smart XL grill.
3. Cover the Ninja Foodi Grill's hood and select the Manual settings.
4. Set the temperature to 350 degrees F and cook on the "Grill" Mode for 1 minute per side.
5. Keep the avocados in the grill with their cut side up and crack one egg into each avocado.
6. Drizzle salt and black pepper on top.
7. Cover the grill's hood and cook for 2 minutes.
8. Serve warm.

Serving Suggestion: Serve the avocado cups with crispy bacon on top.

Variation Tip: Top egg with chopped fresh herbs.

Nutritional Information Per Serving:

Calories 322 | Fat 12g |Sodium 202mg | Carbs 4.6g | Fiber 4g | Sugar 8g | Protein 17.3g

Poultry Recipes

Baja-Style Rosemary Chicken Skewers

Prep Time: 15 minutes.

Cook Time: 10 minutes.

Serves: 4

Ingredients:

- 1/2 small white onion, chopped
- 3 garlic cloves, minced
- 2 dried chiles de arbol, crumbled
- 1 teaspoon minced rosemary
- 1 teaspoon dried Mexican oregano, crumbled
- 1/4 cup lemon juice
- 1/4 cup olive oil
- 2 lbs. boneless chicken thighs, cut into pieces
- Salt, to taste
- Black pepper, to taste
- Lime wedges, for serving

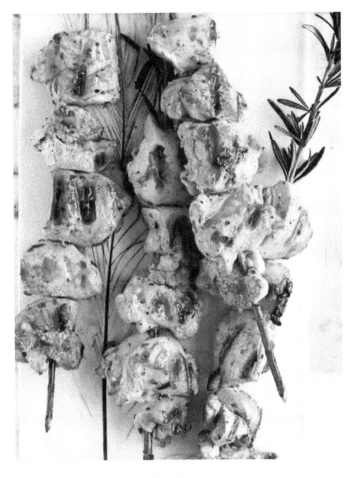

Preparation:

1. Blend garlic with the rest of the spices and herbs in a blender.
2. Rub this mixture over the chicken pieces then thread these pieces over wooden skewers.
3. Place the chicken skewers in the Ninja Foodi Smart XL grill.
4. Cover the Ninja Foodi Grill's hood and select the Manual settings.
5. Set the temperature to 350 degrees F and cook on the "Grill" Mode for 5 minutes per side.
6. Serve warm.

Serving Suggestion: Serve the skewers with mayonnaise dip.

Variation Tip: Add shredded cheese on top of the grilled skewers.

Nutritional Information Per Serving:

Calories 380 | Fat 19g |Sodium 318mg | Carbs 9g | Fiber 5g | Sugar 3g | Protein 26g

Big Bob Gibson's Chicken

Prep Time: 15 minutes.

Cook Time: 20 minutes.

Serves: 6

Ingredients:

- 1 (3 ½-lb.) chicken, cut into pieces
- Vegetable oil, for brushing
- Salt and black pepper, to taste
- 1 cup mayonnaise
- 1/2 cup white vinegar
- 1/4 cup chicken broth
- 1 teaspoon prepared horseradish
- 1 teaspoon lemon juice
- 1/4 teaspoon cayenne pepper

Preparation:

1. Mix mayo with black pepper, vinegar, broth, horseradish, lemon juice and cayenne pepper in a bowl.
2. Liberally brush this mixture over the chicken pieces.
3. Place the chicken pieces in the Ninja Foodi Smart XL grill.
4. Cover the Ninja Foodi Grill's hood and select the Manual settings.
5. Set the temperature to 350 degrees F and cook on the "Grill" Mode for 5-10 minutes per side.
6. Serve warm.

Serving Suggestion: Serve the chicken with yogurt sauce.

Variation Tip: Coat the chicken with parmesan before cooking.

Nutritional Information Per Serving:

Calories 404 | Fat 13g |Sodium 216mg | Carbs 7g | Fiber 3g | Sugar 4g | Protein 31g

Grilled Chicken and Radishes

Prep Time: 15 minutes.

Cook Time: 14 minutes.

Serves: 6

Ingredients:

- 3 lb. boneless chicken thighs
- 3 1/2 teaspoon salt
- 1 (12-ounces) can ginger beer
- 6 garlic cloves, grated
- 3/4 cup 6 tablespoons rice vinegar
- 3 tablespoons 1 teaspoon ginger, grated
- 1 tablespoon white miso
- 3/4 cup 1 tablespoon vegetable oil

To Serve

- 6 scallions, chopped
- 2 bunches radishes, halved
- Black pepper, to taste
- 3 heads lettuce, leaves separated

Preparation:

1. Mix ginger beer with the rest of the ingredients for chicken in a bowl.
2. Cover and marinate the chicken for 1 hour in the refrigerator.
3. Place the chicken in the Ninja Foodi Smart XL grill.
4. Cover the Ninja Foodi Grill's hood and select the Manual settings.
5. Set the temperature to 350 degrees F and cook on the "Grill" Mode for 7 minutes per side.
6. Meanwhile toss radishes with scallions, and black pepper.
7. Serve the grilled chicken with radishes mixture and lettuce leaves.

Serving Suggestion: Serve the chicken with cucumber salad.

Variation Tip: Add brussels sprouts to the meal.

Nutritional Information Per Serving:

Calories 348 | Fat 12g |Sodium 710mg | Carbs 4g | Fiber 5g | Sugar 3g | Protein 31g

Grilled Chicken with Olives

Prep Time: 15 minutes.

Cook Time: 14 minutes.

Serves: 4

Ingredients:

- 3 tablespoons 1/2 cup olive oil
- 4 boneless chicken breasts
- Salt, to taste,
- Black pepper, to taste
- 2 lemons
- 4 garlic cloves, crushed
- 3 large sprigs thyme
- 1 cup torn pitted Castelvetrano olives, chopped

Preparation:

1. Mix lemon juice with the rest of the ingredients in a large bowl.
2. Cover and marinate the chicken for 30 minutes in the refrigerator.
3. Place the chicken in the Ninja Foodi Smart XL grill.
4. Cover the Ninja Foodi Grill's hood and select the Manual settings.
5. Set the temperature to 350 degrees F and cook on the "Grill" Mode for 7 minutes per side.
6. Slice the chicken and serve warm with remaining marinade on top.

Serving Suggestion: Serve the chicken with yogurt dip and peas snaps.

Variation Tip: Add grilled zucchini to the recipe as well.

Nutritional Information Per Serving:

Calories 375 | Fat 16g |Sodium 255mg | Carbs 4.1g | Fiber 1.2g | Sugar 5g | Protein 24.1g

Piri Piri Chicken

Prep Time: 15 minutes.

Cook Time: 10 minutes.

Serves: 3

Ingredients:

- 1 small red bell pepper, chopped
- 1/2 cup fresh cilantro leaves
- 1 small shallot, chopped
- 2 tablespoons red wine vinegar
- 2 tablespoons olive oil
- 1 tablespoon paprika
- 2 garlic cloves, crushed
- 2 piri piri chiles, stemmed
- 1 1/2 teaspoon dried oregano
- 1 tablespoon salt, to taste
- 1 1/4 lbs. boneless chicken thighs, cut into 1-inch pieces
- Canola oil, for brushing
- 1 lb. Shishito peppers

Preparation:

1. Blend peppers with vinegar, garlic and other ingredients in a blender.
2. Add this marinade and chicken to a large bowl.
3. Cover and marinate the chicken for 30 minutes in the refrigerator.
4. Place the chicken in the Ninja Foodi Smart XL grill.
5. Cover the Ninja Foodi Grill's hood and select the Manual settings.
6. Set the temperature to 350 degrees F and cook on the "Grill" Mode for 5 minutes per side.
7. Serve warm.

Serving Suggestion: Serve the chicken with fried cauliflower rice.

Variation Tip: You can add dried herbs for seasoning as well.

Nutritional Information Per Serving:

Calories 373 | Fat 8g |Sodium 146mg | Carbs 8g | Fiber 5g | Sugar 1g | Protein 23g

Grilled Chicken Breasts with Lemon

Prep Time: 15 minutes.

Cook Time: 16 minutes.

Serves: 4

Ingredients:

- 1 1/2 tablespoon lemon juice
- 1/4 teaspoon dried thyme
- 1/2 teaspoon dried red-pepper flakes
- 1 garlic clove, minced
- 1/4 cup olive oil
- 1/4 teaspoon salt
- 1/4 teaspoon black pepper
- 4 bone-in chicken breasts

Preparation:

1. Mix lemon juice with thyme, red pepper flakes, garlic, salt, black pepper and oil in a small bowl.
2. Liberally brush this mixture over the chicken pieces.
3. Place the chicken in the Ninja Foodi Smart XL grill.
4. Cover the Ninja Foodi Grill's hood and select the Manual settings.
5. Set the temperature to 350 degrees F and cook on the "Grill" Mode for 8 minutes per side.
6. Serve warm.

Serving Suggestion: Serve the grilled chicken with cucumber dip.

Variation Tip: Drizzle dried herbs on top and press before grilling.

Nutritional Information Per Serving:

Calories 357 | Fat 12g |Sodium 48mg | Carbs 6g | Fiber 2g | Sugar 0g | Protein 24g

Grilled Chicken with Mustard Sauce

Prep Time: 15 minutes.

Cook Time: 12 minutes.

Serves: 8

Ingredients:

- 3/4 cup choc zero maple syrup
- 1/2 cup pure olive oil
- 1/2 cup ruby port
- 2 tablespoons Dijon mustard
- 2 tablespoons soy sauce
- 2 tablespoons black pepper
- 1 tablespoon Worcestershire sauce
- 1 shallot, minced
- 4 (3-lbs.) chicken, cut into quarters

Preparation:

1. Mix mustard with the rest of the ingredients in a large bowl, except chicken.
2. Stir in chicken, mix well to coat, cover and marinate for 30 minutes in the refrigerator.
3. Place the chicken in the Ninja Foodi Smart XL grill.
4. Cover the Ninja Foodi Grill's hood and select the Manual settings.
5. Set the temperature to 350 degrees F and cook on the "Grill" Mode for 6 minutes per side.
6. Serve warm.

Serving Suggestion: Serve the chicken with roasted cauliflower mash.

Variation Tip: Add some Sugar-free BBQ sauce to the seasoning.

Nutritional Information Per Serving:

Calories 329 | Fat 5g |Sodium 510mg | Carbs 7g | Fiber 5g | Sugar 4g | Protein 21g

Grilled Chicken with Chimichurri

Prep Time: 15 minutes.

Cook Time: 10 minutes.

Serves: 12

Ingredients:

- 2 (4-lbs.) whole chickens, cut into pieces.

Chimichurri

- 1 cup olive oil
- 1 bunch cilantro, leaves chopped
- 1/2 bunch parsley, chopped
- 3 tablespoons garlic, minced
- 3 tablespoons lemon juice
- 3 tablespoons shallot, chopped
- 2 1/4 teaspoon fresh oregano leaves
- 1 1/2 teaspoon Salt, to taste
- 1 1/2 teaspoon balsamic vinegar

SPICE BLEND

- 5 teaspoons paprika
- 4 teaspoons salt, to taste
- 1 tablespoon ancho chile powder

- 1 teaspoon crushed chile de árbol

- 2 teaspoons dried Mexican oregano
- 1 teaspoon chipotle chile powder

Preparation:

1. Mix all the spices in a bowl and rub them liberally over the chicken.
2. Place the chicken in the Ninja Foodi Smart XL grill.
3. Cover the Ninja Foodi Grill's hood and select the Manual settings.
4. Set the temperature to 375 degrees F and cook on the "Grill" Mode for 5 minutes per side.
5. Meanwhile, blend all the chimichurri ingredients in a blender.
6. Pour this sauce over the grilled chicken and serve.

Serving Suggestion: Serve the chicken with warm keto bread.

Variation Tip: Add a pinch of erythritol to season the fish mildly sweet.

Nutritional Information Per Serving:

Calories 382 | Fat 4g |Sodium 232mg | Carbs 4g | Fiber 1g | Sugar 0g | Protein 21g

Tamarind-Glazed Chicken Wings

Prep Time: 15 minutes.

Cook Time: 20 minutes.

Serves: 8

Ingredients:

- ¾ cup tamarind purée
- ¼ cup fish sauce
- 2 tablespoons erythritol
- 1 tablespoon crushed red pepper flakes
- 1 teaspoon ground cumin
- 3 teaspoons Diamond Crystal salt
- 4 lb. chicken wings
- ¼ small red onion, sliced
- Cilantro leaves with tender stems and lime

wedges

Preparation:

1. Blend tamarind puree with fish sauce, red pepper flakes, cumin, salt, red onion, and sweetener in a blender.
2. Mix this marinade with chicken wings in a bowl.
3. Cover and marinate for 30 minutes in the refrigerator.
4. Place the chicken in the Ninja Foodi Smart XL grill.
5. Cover the Ninja Foodi Grill's hood and select the Manual settings.
6. Set the temperature to 350 degrees F and cook on the "Grill" Mode for 10 minutes per side.
7. Serve warm.

Serving Suggestion: Serve the chicken with a kale salad on the side.

Variation Tip: Add lemon juice for a refreshing taste.

Nutritional Information Per Serving:

Calories 335 | Fat 25g |Sodium 122mg | Carbs 3g | Fiber 0.4g | Sugar 1g | Protein 33g

Grilled Chicken Thighs

Prep Time: 15 minutes.

Cook Time: 14 minutes.

Serves: 3

Ingredients:

- 1/4 cup lemongrass, chopped
- 3 tablespoons shallot, chopped
- 1 ½ tablespoons granulated erythritol
- 1 ½ tablespoons canola oil
- 1 ½ tablespoons fish sauce
- 1 tablespoon garlic, chopped
- 1 teaspoon soy sauce
- 3/8 teaspoon cayenne pepper
- 1 ¼ lbs. boneless chicken thighs

Preparation:

1. Mix lemongrass with shallots and the rest of the ingredients in a bowl.
2. Add chicken, rub it well then cover and marinate for 30 minutes in the refrigerator.
3. Place the chicken in the Ninja Foodi Smart XL grill.
4. Cover the Ninja Foodi Grill's hood and select the Manual settings.
5. Set the temperature to 350 degrees F and cook on the "Grill" Mode for 7 minutes per side.
6. Serve warm.

Serving Suggestion: Serve the chicken with fresh kale salad.

Variation Tip: Add shredded cheese to the chicken.

Nutritional Information Per Serving:

Calories 440 | Fat 5g |Sodium 244mg | Carbs 6g | Fiber 1g | Sugar 1g | Protein 27g

Garlicky Lemongrass Chicken

Prep Time: 15 minutes.

Cook Time: 14 minutes.

Serves: 8

Ingredients:

- 5 plump lemongrass stalks, bulb, chopped
- 3 scallions, chopped
- 1 large garlic clove, smashed
- 1 large jalapeño, chopped
- Pinch of erythritol
- 1/4 cup vegetable oil
- Salt and black pepper, to taste
- 4 lbs. boneless chicken thighs and breasts

Preparation:

1. Blend lemon grass with the rest of the ingredients except chicken in a food processor.
2. Rub this mixture over the chicken liberally.
3. Place the chicken in the Ninja Foodi Smart XL grill.
4. Cover the Ninja Foodi Grill's hood and select the Manual settings.
5. Set the temperature to 350 degrees F and cook on the "Grill" Mode for 7 minutes per side.
6. Serve warm.

Serving Suggestion: Serve the chicken with parsley on top.

Variation Tip: Coat the chicken with lemon juice for good taste.

Nutritional Information Per Serving:

Calories 418 | Fat 22g |Sodium 350mg | Carbs 2.2g | Fiber 0.7g | Sugar 1g | Protein 24.3g

Grilled Red Curry Chicken

Prep Time: 15 minutes.

Cook Time: 14 minutes.

Serves: 6

Ingredients:

- 1 (3-lbs.) chicken, cut into pieces
- 1/4 cup unsweetened coconut milk
- 2 tablespoons red curry paste
- 1 teaspoon erythritol
- Salt and black pepper, to taste

Preparation:

1. Mix chicken pieces with salt and black pepper in a bowl.
2. Place the chicken in the Ninja Foodi Smart XL grill.
3. Cover the Ninja Foodi Grill's hood and select the Manual settings.
4. Set the temperature to 350 degrees F and cook on the "Grill" Mode for 7 minutes per side.
5. Meanwhile, cook coconut milk with curry paste and sweetener in a saucepan on medium-low heat until its thick,
6. Toss in grilled chicken pieces and mix well to coat.
7. Serve warm.

Serving Suggestion: Serve the chicken with garlic butter and sautéed broccoli.

Variation Tip: Drizzle paprika on top for more spice.

Nutritional Information Per Serving:

Calories 401 | Fat 7g |Sodium 269mg | Carbs 5g | Fiber 4g | Sugar 12g | Protein 26g

Beef and Lamb Recipes

Grilled Bone-In Rib Eye

Prep Time: 15 minutes.

Cook Time: 10 minutes.

Serves: 6

Ingredients:

- 3 (2-inch) bone-in rib-eye steaks
- Salt and black pepper, to taste
- Flaky sea salt, for serving

Preparation:

1. Pat fry dry the steaks and rub with black pepper and salt.
2. Cover and refrigerate for 1 hour.
3. Place the steak in the Ninja Foodi Smart XL grill.
4. Cover the Ninja Foodi Grill's hood and select the Manual settings.
5. Set the temperature to 350 degrees F and cook on the "Grill" Mode for 5 minutes per side.
6. Slice and transfer the steak to a plate
7. Serve warm.

Serving Suggestion: Serve the beef with steaming cauliflower rice.

Variation Tip: Add 1 tablespoon lemon juice to the seasoning and marinate.

Nutritional Information Per Serving:

Calories 361 | Fat 16g |Sodium 189mg | Carbs 3g | Fiber 0.3g | Sugar 18.2g | Protein 33.3g

Coconut-Marinated Short Rib Kebabs

Prep Time: 11 minutes.

Cook Time: 15 minutes.

Serves: 3

Ingredients:

PEANUT-CHILE OIL

- 1 lemongrass stalk
- 1 large shallot, chopped
- 2 garlic cloves, chopped
- 1-inch piece ginger, peeled, chopped
- ½ cup vegetable oil
- ½ teaspoon salt, to taste
- 4 New Mexico chiles, seeds removed, flesh torn
- 1 teaspoon crushed red pepper flakes
- ¼ cup crushed salted, roasted peanuts
- 2 teaspoons fish sauce

SHORT RIBS

- 1¼ lbs. boneless beef short ribs
- 1 lemongrass stalk
- 2 garlic cloves, grated
- 2-inch piece ginger, peeled, grated
- ¾ cup unsweetened coconut milk
- 2 tablespoons fish sauce
- 2 tablespoons erythritol
- 1 tablespoon fresh lime juice
- 1 teaspoon ground turmeric
- Vegetable oil (for grill)
- Salt, to taste

Preparation:

1. Cook lemongrass, salt, oil, ginger, garlic and shallot in a saucepan until soft.
2. Remove from the heat then add red pepper flakes and chiles.
3. Puree this mixture in a blender until smooth then transfer to a bowl.

4. Stir in fish sauce and peanuts.

5. Mix rest of the ingredients with short ribs in a ziplock bag and seal.

6. Marinate the short ribs in the refrigerator for 2 hours.

7. Place the ribs in the Ninja Foodi Smart XL grill.

8. Cover the Ninja Foodi Grill's hood and select the Manual settings.

9. Set the temperature to 350 degrees F and cook on the "Grill" Mode for 5 minutes per side.

10. Serve warm

Serving Suggestion: Serve the kebabs with a fresh spinach salad.

Variation Tip: Add a drizzle of cheese on top of the skewers after grilling.

Nutritional Information Per Serving:

Calories 445 | Fat 7.9g |Sodium 581mg | Carbs 4g | Fiber 2.6g | Sugar 0.1g | Protein 42.5g

Hasselback Short Rib Bulgogi

Prep Time: 15 minutes.

Cook Time: 14 minutes.

Serves: 3

Ingredients:

SSAMJANG

- 1 scallion, chopped
- ¼ cup white miso
- 1 teaspoon gochujang (Korean hot pepper paste)
- 1 teaspoon erythritol
- 1 teaspoon toasted sesame oil
- 1 teaspoon toasted sesame seeds

SCALLION SALAD

- 6 scallions
- 2 teaspoons toasted sesame oil
- 2 teaspoons unseasoned rice vinegar
- 1 teaspoon toasted sesame seeds

SHORT RIBS

- 1"-piece ginger, peeled, grated
- 2 garlic cloves, grated
- ¼ cup soy sauce
- 2 tablespoons unseasoned rice vinegar
- 2 tablespoons erythritol
- 1 tablespoon gochugaru (Korean red pepper powder)
- 1 tablespoon toasted sesame oil
- 1½ lb. boneless beef short ribs, trimmed
- Salt, to taste
- Lettuce leaves, for serving

Preparation:

1. Mix all the ingredients for Ssamjang in a bowl.
2. Toss the scallion salad ingredients in a suitable salad bowl and cover to refrigerate until ready to serve.

3. Mix short ribs with the rest of the spices and ingredients in a bowl.

4. Cover and marinate for 1-3 hours in the refrigerator.

5. Place the ribs in the Ninja Foodi Smart XL grill.

6. Cover the Ninja Foodi Grill's hood and select the Manual settings.

7. Set the temperature to 350 degrees F and cook on the "Grill" Mode for 7 minutes per side.

8. Pour the prepared Ssamjang on top and serve warm with scallion salad.

9. Enjoy.

Serving Suggestion: Serve the beef with roasted veggies.

Variation Tip: Use toasted sesame seeds for garnishing.

Nutritional Information Per Serving:

Calories 384 | Fat 25g |Sodium 460mg | Carbs 6g | Fiber 0.4g | Sugar 2g | Protein 26g

Grilled Beef with Broccoli

Prep Time: 10 minutes.

Cook Time: 20 minutes.

Serves: 3

Ingredients:

- 6 garlic cloves, grated
- 3-inch piece ginger, peeled, grated
- ¾ cup oyster sauce
- ¾ cup Shaoxing wine
- ¾ cup soy sauce
- ¼ cup toasted sesame oil
- 3 tablespoons unseasoned rice vinegar
- 1½ lbs. flank steak
- 2 medium heads of broccoli, cut into florets
- Sliced scallions, toasted sesame seeds, to serve

Preparation:

1. Mix vinegar, oil, soy sauce, wine, oyster sauce, ginger and garlic in a medium bowl.
2. Add 2 cups marinade and steak to a ziplock bag, seal and refrigerate for 1 hour.
3. Place the steak in the Ninja Foodi Smart XL grill.
4. Cover the Ninja Foodi Grill's hood and select the Manual settings.
5. Set the temperature to 350 degrees F and cook on the "Grill" Mode for 5 minutes per side.
6. Slice and transfer this steak to a plate.
7. Mix remaining marinade with broccoli in a bowl.
8. Grill the broccoli florets for 5-6 minutes per side.
9. Add broccoli to the steak then garnish with sesame seeds and scallions.
10. Serve warm

Serving Suggestion: Serve the beef with steamed cauliflower rice.

Variation Tip: Add butter sauce on top of the beef before cooking.

Nutritional Information Per Serving:

Calories 419 | Fat 13g |Sodium 432mg | Carbs 9.1g | Fiber 3g | Sugar 1g | Protein 33g

Skirt Steak with Ba Sauce

Prep Time: 15 minutes.

Cook Time: 10 minutes.

Serves: 2

Ingredients:

SAUCE

- 2 tablespoons balsamic vinegar
- 2 tablespoons Worcestershire sauce
- 2 tablespoons sugar-free ketchup
- 1 tablespoon olive oil
- 1 tablespoon vinegar-based hot sauce
- 1 teaspoon Dijon mustard
- 1 teaspoon choc-zero maple syrup
- Salt, to taste

STEAK

- 1½ lb. skirt steak, cut into 4"–5" pieces
- Salt and black pepper, to taste
- Flaky sea salt

Preparation:

1. Mix 1 tablespoon water, mustard, choc-zero maple syrup, hot sauce, oil, ketchup, Worcestershire sauce, salt and vinegar in a bowl.
2. Rub the steak with black pepper and salt liberally.
3. Place the steak in the Ninja Foodi Smart XL grill.
4. Cover the Ninja Foodi Grill's hood and select the Manual settings.
5. Set the temperature to 350 degrees F and cook on the "Grill" Mode for 5 minutes per side.
6. Slice and transfer the steak to a plate and pour the prepared sauce on top.
7. Serve warm.

Serving Suggestion: Serve the steak with fresh herbs on top and a bowl of steamed cauliflower rice.

Variation Tip: You can also use dry mustard powder instead of Dijon mustard.

Nutritional Information Per Serving:

Calories 388 | Fat 8g |Sodium 611mg | Carbs 8g | Fiber 0g | Sugar 4g | Protein 13g

Coconut and Lemongrass Steak Skewers

Prep Time: 10 minutes.

Cook Time: 8 minutes.

Serves: 3

Ingredients:

DRESSING

- 2 serrano chiles, chopped
- ¼ cup fresh lime juice
- 2 tablespoons olive oil
- 2 tablespoons red onion, chopped
- 2 teaspoons choc-zero maple syrup
- Salt, to taste

SKEWERS

- 2 lemongrass stalks, sliced
- 2 serrano chiles, with seeds if you want some heat
- 1 2"-piece ginger, peeled, sliced
- 4 garlic cloves
- 1 (13 ½ -ounces) can unsweetened coconut milk
- ⅓ cup seasoned rice vinegar
- 1½ lb. trimmed hanger steak, cut into 1" cubes
- Salt, to taste
- Chopped cilantro (for serving)

Preparation:

1. Mix all the dressing ingredients in a bowl.
2. Blend coconut milk with vinegar, garlic, ginger, chiles and lemongrass in a blender until smooth.
3. Mix meat with this lemongrass marinade in a bowl.
4. Cover and refrigerate this meat for 4 hours.
5. Thread the marinated meat on the wooden skewers.
6. Place the skewers in the Ninja Foodi Smart XL grill.
7. Cover the Ninja Foodi Grill's hood and select the Manual settings.
8. Set the temperature to 350 degrees F and cook on the "Grill" Mode for 4 minutes per side.
9. Pour the dressing over the skewers and garnish with cilantro.
10. Serve warm.

Serving Suggestion: Serve the skewers with roasted green beans and mashed cauliflower.

Variation Tip: Add chopped sautéed kale on top before serving.

Nutritional Information Per Serving:

Calories 429 | Fat 17g |Sodium 422mg | Carbs 5g | Fiber 0g | Sugar 1g | Protein 41g

Grilled Brisket with Scallion-Peanut Salsa

Prep Time: 15 minutes.

Cook Time: 28 minutes.

Serves: 3

Ingredients:

MEAT

- 1½ lb. flat-cut beef brisket, ¼" thick
- 4 garlic cloves, grated
- ¼ cup fresh lime juice
- ¼ cup oyster sauce
- 2 tablespoons soy sauce
- 2 tablespoons erythritol
- 2 teaspoons toasted sesame oil

SALSA

- Vegetable oil, for grill
- ⅓ cup olive oil
- ⅓ cup raw peanuts, chopped
- 1 garlic clove, grated
- 2 teaspoons toasted sesame seeds
- 1 teaspoon crushed red pepper flakes
- 2 tablespoons fresh lime juice
- 2 teaspoons choc-zero maple syrup
- Salt, to taste
- 1 bunch scallions, sliced into matchsticks
- ½ bunch cilantro, torn into sprigs

Preparation:

1. Slice the brisket into ½ inch thick slices.
2. Mix them with garlic, oil, erythritol, soy sauce, lime juice and oyster sauce in a small bowl.
3. Cover and marinate the brisket in the refrigerator for 1 hour.
4. Place the brisket in the Ninja Foodi Smart XL grill.
5. Cover the Ninja Foodi Grill's hood and select the Manual settings.
6. Set the temperature to 350 degrees F and cook on the "Grill" Mode for 5-10 minutes per side.

7. Meanwhile, Sauté peanuts with oil in a saucepan over medium heat for 8 minutes.

8. Remove them from the heat then add rest of the ingredients.

9. Serve the brisket slices with the peanut salsa.

Serving Suggestion: Serve the beef with avocado guacamole and cauliflower rice.

Variation Tip: Add sweet paprika for a tangy taste.

Nutritional Information Per Serving:

Calories 440 | Fat 14g |Sodium 220mg | Carbs 2g | Fiber 0.2g | Sugar 1g | Protein 37g

Lacquered Rib Eye

Prep Time: 10 minutes.

Cook Time: 18 minutes.

Serves: 4

Ingredients:

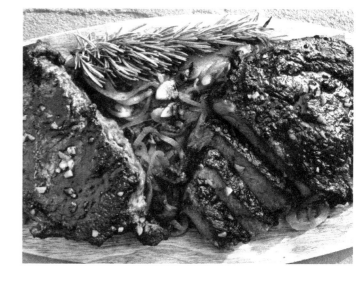

- ¼ cup sherry vinegar
- 2 tablespoons soy sauce
- 1 tablespoon fish sauce
- 2 teaspoons erythritol
- 1 garlic clove, crushed
- Vegetable oil (for grill)
- 2–2½-lb. bone-in rib eye (2" thick)
- Salt, to taste
- Lemon wedges, for serving

Preparation:

1. Boil garlic, sweetener, fish sauce, soy sauce and vinegar in a small pan and cook for 8 minutes on a simmer until reduced to half.
2. Rub the steak with salt and black pepper liberally.
3. Place the steaks in the Ninja Foodi Smart XL grill.
4. Cover the Ninja Foodi Grill's hood and select the Manual settings.
5. Set the temperature to 400 degrees F and cook on the "Grill" Mode for 5 minutes.
6. Brush the prepared sauce over the steaks liberally.
7. Grill for another 5 minutes then slice and serve warm with lemon wedges on top.

Serving Suggestion: Serve the steaks with fresh cucumber salad.

Variation Tip: Toss the beef with the pork rinds before cooking.

Nutritional Information Per Serving:

Calories 352 | Fat 2.4g |Sodium 216mg | Carbs 6g | Fiber 2.3g | Sugar 1.2g | Protein 27g

Tri-Tip Steak with Tiger Bite Sauce

Prep Time: 15 minutes.

Cook Time: 15 minutes.

Serves: 2

Ingredients:

STEAK

- 2 tablespoons Sichuan peppercorns
- 2 tablespoons coriander seeds
- 1 tablespoon cumin seeds
- 2 (1-lb.) sirloin steaks
- ¼ cup vegetable oil
- 3 tablespoons oyster sauce
- 1 tablespoon fish sauce

SAUCE

- 1½ cups cherry tomatoes
- 1 teaspoon vegetable oil
- 1 small shallot, chopped
- 4 garlic cloves, chopped
- 4 Thai chiles, chopped
- ½ cup cilantro, chopped
- 1 tablespoon fish sauce
- 1 tablespoon oyster sauce

Preparation:

1. Toast cumin seeds, coriander seeds and Sichuan peppercorns in a dry skillet for 3 minutes then grind them in a grinder.
2. Rub the stead with salt, spices, oyster sauce, oil, and fish in a bowl.
3. Cover and refrigerate for 4 hours.
4. Place the steak in the Ninja Foodi Smart XL grill.
5. Cover the Ninja Foodi Grill's hood and select the Manual settings.
6. Set the temperature to 350 degrees F and cook on the "Grill" Mode for 5 minutes per side.
7. Slice and transfer the steak to a platter.
8. Mix tomatoes with oil and salt and grill them in the Ninja Foodi XL grill for 5 minutes.

9. Blend salt, chiles, garlic, cilantro and shallots in a blender until smooth.

10. Mix tomatoes with shallot mixture and the rest of the ingredients in a bowl.

11. Pour this sauce over the steak and serve warm.

Serving Suggestion: Serve the steaks with toasted keto bread slices and cabbage slaw.

Variation Tip: Add canned adobo peppers to season the steaks.

Nutritional Information Per Serving:

Calories 301 | Fat 16g |Sodium 412mg | Carbs 3g | Fiber 0.2g | Sugar 1g | Protein 28.2g

Hawaiian Rib-Eye Steak

Prep Time: 15 minutes.

Cook Time: 10 minutes.

Serves: 2

Ingredients:

STEAK

- 2 cups chicken broth
- 2 tablespoon lemon juice
- ½ cup soy sauce
- ½ cup erythritol
- 5 tablespoons apple cider vinegar
- 2 teaspoons toasted sesame oil
- ⅓ cup white onion, chopped
- 1-inch piece ginger, peeled, chopped
- 2 (1-inch) thick bone-in rib-eye steaks

BUTTER

- 4 tablespoons unsalted butter, room temperature
- 2 teaspoons toasted sesame oil
- Salt, to taste

Preparation:

1. Mix soy sauce, erythritol, lemon juice, water, vinegar, oil, onion and ginger in a bowl
2. Keep 2 tablespoons of this marinade for butter.
3. Transfer remaining marinade and steak to a large ziplock bag.
4. Seal and refrigerate the steak for 1 hour.
5. Meanwhile, mix butter with oil, salt and remaining marinade a bowl.
6. Pour the mixture at the centre of the parchment paper sheet and roll it into a log.
7. Seal both the ends and refrigerate the butter for 1 hour.
8. Place the steak in the Ninja Foodi Smart XL grill.
9. Cover the Ninja Foodi Grill's hood and select the Manual settings.
10. Set the temperature to 350 degrees F and cook on the "Grill" Mode for 5 minutes per side.
11. Slice and transfer the steak to a plate.
12. Cut the butter log into thick slices and add them on top of the steak.

13. Serve warm.

Serving Suggestion: Serve the steak with roasted veggies on the side.

Variation Tip: Add sweet paprika for more taste.

Nutritional Information Per Serving:

Calories 334 | Fat 16g |Sodium 462mg | Carbs 3g | Fiber 0.4g | Sugar 3g | Protein 35.3g

Soy Sauce–Marinated Grilled Flank Steak

Prep Time: 15 minutes.

Cook Time: 14 minutes.

Serves: 2

Ingredients:

- 3 tablespoons olive oil
- 1½ lb. flank steak
- Salt and black pepper, to taste
- 1 bunch scallions, trimmed
- ¼ cup mirin
- ¼ cup soy sauce
- 2 tablespoons erythritol
- 1 tablespoon distilled white vinegar
- 1 tablespoon Sriracha
- 2 teaspoons toasted sesame oil
- Toasted sesame seeds, for serving

Preparation:

1. Mix all the ingredients with steaks in a large bowl.
2. Cover and refrigerate for 4 hours in the refrigerator.
3. Place the steaks in the Ninja Foodi Smart XL grill.
4. Cover the Ninja Foodi Grill's hood and select the Manual settings.
5. Set the temperature to 375 degrees F and cook on the "Grill" Mode for 7 minutes per side.
6. Slice and serve warm.

Serving Suggestion: Serve the chicken with sesame seeds and scallions on top.

Variation Tip: Add 1 tablespoon lime juice to the seasoning.

Nutritional Information Per Serving:

Calories 431 | Fat 20.1g |Sodium 364mg | Carbs 3g | Fiber 1g | Sugar 1.4g | Protein 15g

Grilled Rib Eye with Shishito Pepper Salsa

Prep Time: 15 minutes.

Cook Time: 10 minutes.

Serves: 6

Ingredients:

- 3 (1½-inch) thick boneless rib eyes
- Salt and black pepper, to taste
- 1¼ cups olive oil
- 1 lb. Shishito peppers
- 2 garlic cloves, grated
- ¼ cup sherry vinegar
- Flaky sea salt

Preparation:

1. Pat fry dry the meat and rub with black pepper and salt.
2. Cover and refrigerate for 1 hour.
3. Place the steak in the Ninja Foodi Smart XL grill.
4. Cover the Ninja Foodi Grill's hood and select the Manual settings.
5. Set the temperature to 350 degrees F and cook on the "Grill" Mode for 5 minutes per side.
6. Slice and transfer the steak to a plate
7. Grill peppers in the Ninja Foodi XL Grill until charred from both the sides.
8. Chop and mix the peppers with the rest of the ingredients.
9. Add this pepper mixture on top of the steak.
10. Serve warm.

Serving Suggestion: Serve the steak with cucumber salad.

Variation Tip: Add 1 tablespoon lime juice to the seasoning and marinate.

Nutritional Information Per Serving:

Calories 380 | Fat 8g |Sodium 339mg | Carbs 5.6g | Fiber 1g | Sugar 2g | Protein 21g

Flank Steak with Zucchini Salsa

Prep Time: 10 minutes.

Cook Time: 10 minutes.

Serves: 3

Ingredients:

- 1½ lbs. zucchini, cut into ¼-inch pieces
- ½ cup red wine vinegar
- 1 tablespoon chopped oregano
- ¼ cup olive oil
- Salt and black pepper, to taste
- 1½-lb. piece flank steak

Preparation:

1. Mix zucchini with vinegar, oregano, olive oil, black pepper and salt in a bowl.
2. Pat fry dry the steak and rub with black pepper and salt.
3. Cover and refrigerate for 1 hour.
4. Place the steak in the Ninja Foodi Smart XL grill.
5. Cover the Ninja Foodi Grill's hood and select the Manual settings.
6. Set the temperature to 350 degrees F and cook on the "Grill" Mode for 5 minutes per side.
7. Slice and transfer the steak to a plate
8. Add the zucchini salsa on top of the steak.
9. Serve warm

Serving Suggestion: Serve the beef with roasted veggies and mashed cauliflower.

Variation Tip: Add dried herbs to the seasoning.

Nutritional Information Per Serving:

Calories 405 | Fat 20g |Sodium 941mg | Carbs 6.1g | Fiber 0.9g | Sugar 0.9g | Protein 45.2g

Pork Recipes

Soy-Based Pork Chops

Prep Time: 15 minutes.

Cook Time: 10 minutes.

Serves: 4

Ingredients:

- 1/4 cup soy sauce
- 1/4 cup unseasoned rice vinegar
- 2 tablespoons erythritol
- 4 (1/2-inch-thick) bone-in pork blade
- Vegetable oil, for grill
- Salt, to taste
- Mint, cilantro and sliced jalapeños, for serving

Preparation:

1. Mix soy sauce, vinegar, and erythritol in a small bowl.
2. Add half of this marinade and pork to a sealable bag.
3. Seal and refrigerate the pork for 1 hour.
4. Place the pork in the Ninja Foodi Smart XL grill.
5. Pour the remaining marinade on top of the pork.
6. Cover the Ninja Foodi Grill's hood and select the Manual settings.
7. Set the temperature to 350 degrees F and cook on the "Grill" Mode for 5 minutes per side.
8. Serve the pork chops with jalapenos and herbs on top.

Serving Suggestion: Serve the chops with cream cheese dip.

Variation Tip: Serve the pork chops on top of a lettuce bed.

Nutritional Information Per Serving:

Calories 376 | Fat 21g |Sodium 476mg | Carbs 2g | Fiber 3g | Sugar 4g | Protein 20g

Barbecue Pork Kebabs

Prep Time: 15 minutes.

Cook Time: 10 minutes.

Serves: 3

Ingredients:

Salsa

- 1/4 large white onion
- 2 jalapeños
- 1/4 cup cilantro, chopped
- 1/4 cup roasted pumpkin seeds, chopped
- 1/4 cup olive oil
- 3 tablespoons fresh lime juice
- Salt, to taste

Pork kebabs

- 1 ¼ lbs. boneless pork shoulder
- 2 tablespoons erythritol
- 2 tablespoons mustard powder
- 2 tablespoons paprika
- 2 teaspoons garlic powder
- 1 teaspoon Black pepper, to taste
- 1/2 teaspoon cayenne pepper
- Vegetable oil, for grill
- Salt, to taste

Preparation:

1. Mix jalapenos and the rest of the ingredients in a bowl, cover and refrigerate until kebabs are ready.
2. Cut the pork into slices and mix them with the rest of the ingredients in a bowl.
3. Thread the pork slices on wooden skewers.
4. Place the pork slices in the Ninja Foodi Smart XL grill.
5. Cover the Ninja Foodi Grill's hood and select the Manual settings.
6. Set the temperature to 350 degrees F and cook on the "Grill" Mode for 5 minutes per side.
7. Serve the skewers with jalapeno salsa.

Serving Suggestion: Serve the kebabs with grilled zucchini salad.

Variation Tip: Add crushed red pepper on top before serving.

Nutritional Information Per Serving:

Calories 380 | Fat 20g |Sodium 686mg | Carbs 3g | Fiber 1g | Sugar 1.2g | Protein 21g

Sweet Grilled Pork Shoulder

Prep Time: 10 minutes.

Cook Time: 20 minutes.

Serves: 8

Ingredients:

Pork:

- 2 garlic heads, cloves peeled
- 1 (wide, 6") piece ginger, peeled, chopped
- 1 cup hoisin sauce
- 3/4 cup fish sauce
- 2/3 cup choc-zero maple syrup
- 2/3 cup Shaoxing (Chinese rice) wine
- 1/2 cup chili oil
- 1/3 cup oyster sauce
- 1/3 cup toasted sesame oil
- 1 (4–5-lb.) boneless pork shoulder, cut into pieces
- Salt, to taste

Preparation:

1. Blend sesame oil, oyster sauce, chili oil, choc-zero maple syrup, wine, fish sauce, hoisin sauce, ginger and garlic in a blender.
2. Keep 1 ½ cups of this mixture in a bowl, cover and refrigerate.
3. Mix the remaining sauce with pork in a sealable bag.
4. Seal and refrigerate the pork for 8 hours.
5. Place the pork in the Ninja Foodi Smart XL grill.
6. Cover the Ninja Foodi Grill's hood and select the Manual settings.
7. Set the temperature to 350 degrees F and cook on the "Grill" Mode for 10 minutes per side.
8. Brush the reserved sauce on top and cook for another 5 minutes.
9. Serve warm.

Serving Suggestion: Serve the pork with mashed cauliflower.

Variation Tip: Dust the pork shoulder with almond flour before grilling for more texture.

Nutritional Information Per Serving:

Calories 391 | Fat 5g |Sodium 88mg | Carbs 3g | Fiber 0g | Sugar 0g | Protein 27g

Pork Chops with Radishes

Prep Time: 15 minutes.

Cook Time: 10 minutes.

Serves: 4

Ingredients:

- 1 tablespoon aniseed or fennel seeds
- 4 (1-inch-thick) bone-in pork chops
- Salt and black pepper, to taste
- 1 teaspoon crushed red pepper flakes
- 3 tablespoons olive oil
- 1 tablespoon lemon juice
- 1 teaspoon rinsed anchovy fillet, chopped
- 3 radishes, trimmed, sliced
- 1/4 cup parsley leaves with tender stems
- 2 bunches scallions, roots trimmed

Preparation:

1. Roast aniseed in a skillet for 2 minutes then grind in a mortar.
2. Rub the aniseed, black pepper, salt and red pepper flakes over the pork chops.
3. Cover and leave these chops for 30 minutes.
4. Place the pork chops in the Ninja Foodi Smart XL grill.
5. Cover the Ninja Foodi Grill's hood and select the Manual settings.
6. Set the temperature to 350 degrees F and cook on the "Grill" Mode for 5 minutes per side.
7. Meanwhile, mix radishes with the rest of the ingredients.
8. Serve the pork chops with radish mixture.
9. Serve.

Serving Suggestion: Serve the pork chops with a kale cucumber salad.

Variation Tip: Add crumbled bacon to the mixture.

Nutritional Information Per Serving:

Calories 325 | Fat 16g |Sodium 431mg | Carbs 2g | Fiber 1.2g | Sugar 4g | Protein 23g

Jalapeño-Marinated Pork Chops

Prep Time: 10 minutes.

Cook Time: 16 minutes.

Serves: 4

Ingredients:

- 1/2 cup 3 tablespoons olive oil
- 4 bone-in pork rib chops
- Salt and black pepper, to taste
- 2 teaspoons coriander seeds
- 1/4 cup apple cider vinegar
- 1 teaspoon erythritol
- 2 large jalapeños
- 1/4 medium white onion, sliced

Preparation:

1. Toast coriander seeds in a skillet for 2 minutes then crush them.
2. Transfer them to a bowl and add erythritol, vinegar, ½ cup oil, black pepper and salt.
3. Mix well and keep this mixture aside.
4. Toss jalapenos with black pepper, salt and 1 tablespoon oil in a bowl.
5. Rub the pork chops with 2 tbsp. oil, black pepper and salt.
6. Place the pork chops in the Ninja Foodi Smart XL grill.
7. Cover the Ninja Foodi Grill's hood and select the Manual settings.
8. Set the temperature to 350 degrees F and cook on the "Grill" Mode for 5 minutes per side.
9. Transfer these chops to a plate.
10. Grill the jalapenos for 2-3 minutes per side.
11. Serve the pork chops with jalapenos and serve warm with onion on top.
12. Enjoy.

Serving Suggestion: Serve the chops with mashed cauliflower.

Variation Tip: Use BBQ sauce for the change of taste.

Nutritional Information Per Serving:

Calories 305 | Fat 25g |Sodium 532mg | Carbs 2.3g | Fiber 0.4g | Sugar 2g | Protein 18.3g

Grilled Pork Shoulder Steaks with Herb Salad

Prep Time: 15 minutes.

Cook Time: 10 minutes.

Serves: 8

Ingredients:

- 4 shallots, chopped
- 6 garlic cloves
- ⅓ cup 3 tablespoons fish sauce
- ⅓ cup 3 tablespoons lime juice
- 3 tablespoons erythritol
- 8 (¾"-thick) pork shoulder steaks
- Salt, to taste
- 2 red Thai chiles, sliced
- 3 cups Thai basil leaves and cilantro leaves, chopped

Preparation:

1. Blend 2 tablespoons erythritol with 1/3 cup lime juice, 1/3 cup fish sauce, garlic and chopped shallots in a blender.
2. Rub the steaks with salt then place in a shallow tray.
3. Pour the prepared sauce over the steaks.
4. Place the steak in the Ninja Foodi Smart XL grill.
5. Cover the Ninja Foodi Grill's hood and select the Manual settings.
6. Set the temperature to 350 degrees F and cook on the "Grill" Mode for 5 minutes per side.
7. Meanwhile, mix rest of the ingredients in a bowl.
8. Slice the grilled steak and serve with this herb salad on top.
9. Enjoy.

Serving Suggestion: Serve the steak with cauliflower cheese casserole.

Variation Tip: Add cheese on top of the pork and then bake after grilling.

Nutritional Information Per Serving:

Calories 425 | Fat 15g |Sodium 345mg | Carbs 2.3g | Fiber 1.4g | Sugar 3g | Protein 23.3g

Habanero-Marinated Pork Chops

Prep Time: 10 minutes.

Cook Time: 16 minutes.

Serves: 4

Ingredients:

- 2 lemongrass stalks
- 1 habanero chile, seeded, chopped
- 2 garlic cloves, crushed
- 1/2 cup water
- 2 tablespoons fish sauce
- 2 tablespoons erythritol
- 6 tablespoons unseasoned rice vinegar
- 4 (1/2"-thick) bone-in pork chops
- 3 tablespoons olive oil
- Salt and black pepper, to taste
- 1 jicama, peeled, sliced
- 1 bunch mustard greens, sliced
- 1/2 cup torn basil leaves

Preparation:

1. Mix lemon grass with 4 tablespoons vinegar, erythritol, fish sauce, water, garlic, and chile in a bowl.
2. Add half of this marinade and pork chops to a sealable bag.
3. Seal the pork chops and refrigerate for 1 hour.
4. Place the pork in the Ninja Foodi Smart XL grill.
5. Cover the Ninja Foodi Grill's hood and select the Manual settings.
6. Set the temperature to 350 degrees F and cook on the "Grill" Mode for 5 minutes per side.
7. Transfer the grilled pork to a plate.
8. Mix jicama with salt and grill for 3 minutes per side.
9. Add the jicama, to the pork.
10. Mix mustard greens with the rest of the ingredients in a bowl.
11. Add the greens to the pork, pour the reserved marinade on top and serve.

Serving Suggestion: Serve the pork chops with boiled cauliflower rice or grilled zucchini.

Variation Tip: Add crushed or sliced almonds to the serving.

Nutritional Information Per Serving:

Calories 361 | Fat 16g |Sodium 515mg | Carbs 9.3g | Fiber 0.1g | Sugar 18.2g | Protein 33.3g

Grilled Pork Ribs with Gochujang Sauce

Prep Time: 15 minutes.

Cook Time: 20 minutes.

Serves: 3

Ingredients:

- 2/3 cup apple cider vinegar
- 1/2 cup erythritol
- 6 tablespoons gochujang (Korean hot pepper paste)
- 1/4 cup adobo
- 2 (4 lb.) racks St. Louis–style pork spareribs
- Salt and black pepper, to taste
- Vegetable oil, for grill

Preparation:

1. Mix vinegar, erythritol, adobo, black pepper, salt and gochujang in a bowl.
2. Brush half of this mixture over the spareribs and reserve and the rest.
3. Place the spareribs in the Ninja Foodi Smart XL grill.
4. Cover the Ninja Foodi Grill's hood and select the Manual settings.
5. Set the temperature to 400 degrees F and cook on the "Grill" Mode for 10 minutes.
6. Rub the remaining sauce over the spareribs and continue cooking for 10 minutes.
7. Serve warm.

Serving Suggestion: Serve these ribs with cauliflower rice.

Variation Tip: Add some Sugar-free BBQ sauce as well for seasoning.

Nutritional Information Per Serving:

Calories 425 | Fat 14g | Sodium 411mg | Carbs 4g | Fiber 0.3g | Sugar 1g | Protein 28.3g

Seafood Recipes

Spicy Grilled Fish

Prep Time: 10 minutes.

Cook Time: 12 minutes.

Serves: 2

Ingredients:

- 1 teaspoon chili powder
- 1 teaspoon dried oregano
- 1/4 teaspoon cayenne pepper
- Salt, to taste
- Black pepper, to taste
- 1 (1 ½ ") thick fillet skin-on white fish
- Lime wedges, for serving

Preparation:

1. Mix chili powder, oregano, cayenne pepper, black pepper and salt in a bowl.
2. Rub this mixture liberally over the white fish.
3. Place the fish in the Ninja Foodi Smart XL grill.
4. Cover the Ninja Foodi Grill's hood and select the Manual settings.
5. Set the temperature to 350 degrees F and cook on the "Grill" Mode for 6 minutes per side.
6. Garnish with lime wedges.
7. Serve warm.

Serving Suggestion: Serve the fish with butter sauce on top.

Variation Tip: Grill the veggies on the side to serve with the fish.

Nutritional Information Per Serving:

Calories 392 | Fat 16g |Sodium 466mg | Carbs 3.9g | Fiber 0.9g | Sugar 0.6g | Protein 48g

Cilantro Lime Grilled Salmon

Prep Time: 15 minutes.

Cook Time: 12 minutes.

Serves: 4

Ingredients:

- 4 (6-ounces) salmon fillets
- Salt, to taste
- Black pepper, to taste
- 4 tablespoons butter
- 1/2 cup lime juice
- 1/4 cup choc-zero maple syrup
- 2 garlic cloves, minced
- 2 tablespoons chopped cilantro

Preparation:

1. Mix butter, salt, black pepper, lime juice, choc-zero maple syrup, and garlic in a bowl.
2. Keep ½ of this marinade aside and add rest to a shallow tray.
3. Add salmon fillets to this marinade, mix well to coat then cover.
4. Refrigerate this salmon for 1 hour.
5. Place the salmon in the Ninja Foodi Smart XL grill.
6. Brush the remaining marinade on top.
7. Cover the Ninja Foodi Grill's hood and select the Manual settings.
8. Set the temperature to 350 degrees F and cook on the "Grill" Mode for 6 minutes per side.
9. Serve warm.

Serving Suggestion: Serve the salmon with sautéed vegetables.

Variation Tip: Use some lemon juice as well for seasoning.

Nutritional Information Per Serving:

Calories 309 | Fat 25g |Sodium 463mg | Carbs 9.9g | Fiber 0.3g | Sugar 0.3g | Protein 18g

Grilled Tilapia with Tomatoes

Prep Time: 15 minutes.

Cook Time: 12 minutes.

Serves: 3

Ingredients:

- 3 tablespoons olive oil
- 2 tablespoons red wine vinegar
- 1/4 small red onion, sliced
- 2 tablespoons fresh oregano leaves
- Salt, to taste
- Black pepper, to taste
- 3 (8-ounces) tilapia filets
- 1/2 cup grape tomatoes

Preparation:

1. Mix red onion with black pepper, salt, oregano, and 2 tablespoons red wine vinegar in a bowl.
2. Brush remaining oil, black pepper and salt over the tilapia fillets.
3. Place the tilapia in the Ninja Foodi Smart XL grill.
4. Cover the Ninja Foodi Grill's hood and select the Manual settings.
5. Set the temperature to 350 degrees F and cook on the "Grill" Mode for 4 minutes per side.
6. Now grill the tomatoes for 4 minutes until blistered.
7. Add the tomatoes to the fish and pour the vinegar mixture on top.
8. Serve warm.

Serving Suggestion: Serve the fish meal on top of the cauliflower rice.

Variation Tip: Add paprika for more spice.

Nutritional Information Per Serving:

Calories 448 | Fat 13g |Sodium 353mg | Carbs 3g | Fiber 0.4g | Sugar 1g | Protein 29g

Lemony Grilled Salmon

Prep Time: 10 minutes.

Cook Time: 10 minutes.

Serves: 4

Ingredients:

- 4 (6-ounces) skin-on salmon fillets
- Olive oil, for brushing
- Salt, to taste
- Black pepper, to taste
- 2 lemons, sliced
- 2 tablespoons butter

Preparation:

1. Rub the salmon with oil, black pepper, and salt.
2. Place the salmon in the Ninja Foodi Smart XL grill.
3. Place the lemon slices on top.
4. Cover the Ninja Foodi Grill's hood and select the Manual settings.
5. Set the temperature to 350 degrees F and cook on the "Grill" Mode for 5 minutes per side.
6. Serve warm.

Serving Suggestion: Serve the salmon with crispy onion rings on the side.

Variation Tip: Add choc-zero maple syrup for seasoning.

Nutritional Information Per Serving:

Calories 376 | Fat 17g |Sodium 1127mg | Carbs 4g | Fiber 1g | Sugar 3g | Protein 29g

Lemon Salmon Skewers

Prep Time: 10 minutes.

Cook Time: 8 minutes.

Serves: 2

Ingredients:

- 1 lb. salmon fillets, cut into 2" pieces
- 3 lemons, sliced
- Olive oil, for brushing
- Salt, to taste
- Black pepper, to taste
- Torn fresh dill, for garnish

Preparation:

1. Thread lemon slices, and salmon cubes on the wooden skewers.
2. Place the skewers in the Ninja Foodi Smart XL grill.
3. Drizzle oil, black pepper and salt on top.
4. Cover the Ninja Foodi Grill's hood and select the Manual settings.
5. Set the temperature to 350 degrees F and cook on the "Grill" Mode for 4 minutes per side.
6. Garnish with dill.
7. Serve warm.

Serving Suggestion: Serve the skewers with yogurt dip.

Variation Tip: Add butter to the fish for more taste.

Nutritional Information Per Serving:

Calories 345 | Fat 36g |Sodium 272mg | Carbs 1g | Fiber 0.2g | Sugar 0.1g | Protein 22.5g

Grilled Halibut with Avocado Salsa

Prep Time: 10 minutes.

Cook Time: 10 minutes.

Serves: 4

Ingredients:

HALIBUT

- 4 (4-6-ounces) halibut steaks
- 2 tablespoons olive oil
- Salt, to taste
- Black pepper, to taste

AVOCADO SALSA

- 1 avocado, peeled and diced
- 1 red pepper, chopped
- 1/2 red onion, diced
- 1 jalapeno, minced
- 1 tablespoon cilantro, chopped
- Juice of 1 lime
- Salt, to taste
- Black pepper, to taste

Preparation:

1. Mix avocado with the rest of the salsa ingredients in a bowl then cover and refrigerate for 15 minutes.
2. Rub halibut steak with oil, black pepper and salt.
3. Place the halibut in the Ninja Foodi Smart XL grill.
4. Cover the Ninja Foodi Grill's hood and select the Manual settings.
5. Set the temperature to 350 degrees F and cook on the "Grill" Mode for 5 minutes per side.
6. Serve the fish with avocado salsa on top.

Serving Suggestion: Serve the halibut with fresh greens and chili sauce on the side.

Variation Tip: Add lemon juice and lemon zest on top before cooking.

Nutritional Information Per Serving:

Calories 457 | Fat 19g |Sodium 557mg | Carbs 9g | Fiber 1.8g | Sugar 1.2g | Protein 32.5g

Spicy Grilled Shrimp

Prep Time: 10 minutes.

Cook Time: 6 minutes.

Serves: 6-8

Ingredients:

- 1/4 cup olive oil
- 1/4 cup lime juice
- 4 garlic cloves, minced
- 3 tablespoons choc-zero maple syrup
- 2 tablespoons soy sauce
- 1 tablespoon chili garlic sauce
- 2 lb. shrimp, peeled and deveined
- 1/4 cup cilantro, chopped
- Lime wedges, for serving

Preparation:

1. Mix oil, lime juice, garlic, choc-zero maple syrup, soy sauce, and chili sauce in a bowl.
2. Keep 1/4 of this marinade aside and add rest to a shallow tray.
3. Add shrimp to this marinade, mix well to coat then cover.
4. Refrigerate these shrimps for 20 minutes.
5. Thread the marinated shrimp over wooden skewers.
6. Place the shrimp in the Ninja Foodi Smart XL grill.
7. Brush the remaining marinade on top.
8. Cover the Ninja Foodi Grill's hood and select the Manual settings.
9. Set the temperature to 350 degrees F and cook on the "Grill" Mode for 3 minutes per side.
10. Garnish with lime wedges and cilantro.
11. Serve warm.

Serving Suggestion: Serve the shrimp with fried cauliflower rice.

Variation Tip: Add some butter sauce on top.

Nutritional Information Per Serving:

Calories 321 | Fat 7.4g |Sodium 356mg | Carbs 9.3g | Fiber 2.4g | Sugar 5g | Protein 37.2g

Hot Shot Salmon

Prep Time: 10 minutes.

Cook Time: 8 minutes.

Serves: 4

Ingredients:

- 1 cup sriracha
- Juice of 2 lemons
- 1/4 cup choc-zero maple syrup
- 4 (6-ounces) salmon fillets
- Chopped fresh chives, for garnish

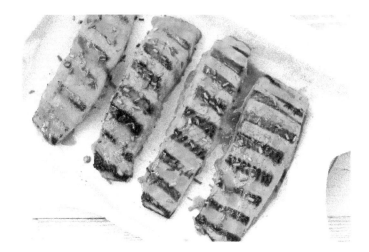

Preparation:

1. Mix sriracha with lemon juice and choc-zero maple syrup in a bowl.
2. Keep ½ of this marinade aside and add rest to a shallow tray.
3. Add salmon fillets to this marinade, mix well to coat then cover.
4. Refrigerate this salmon for 3 hours.
5. Place the salmon in the Ninja Foodi Smart XL grill.
6. Brush the remaining marinade on top.
7. Cover the Ninja Foodi Grill's hood and select the Manual settings.
8. Set the temperature to 350 degrees F and cook on the "Grill" Mode for 4 minutes per side.
9. Serve warm.

Serving Suggestion: Serve the salmon with sautéed green beans and mashed cauliflower.

Variation Tip: Drizzle cheese on top before serving.

Nutritional Information Per Serving:

Calories 395 | Fat 9.5g |Sodium 655mg | Carbs 3.4g | Fiber 0.4g | Sugar 0.4g | Protein 28.3g

Grilled Lobster Tail

Prep Time: 10 minutes.

Cook Time: 11 minutes.

Serves: 4

Ingredients:

- 1/4 cup melted butter
- 1 tablespoon lemon juice
- 1/2 teaspoon lemon zest
- 2 tablespoons chives, chopped
- 2 tablespoons parsley, chopped
- 1 garlic clove, minced
- 1/4 teaspoon salt
- 4 (8-ounces) lobster tails
- olive oil, for brushing
- Black pepper, to taste
- Pinch of crushed red pepper flakes
- Lemon wedges, for serving

Preparation:

1. Cut the lobster tail from top.
2. Mix melted butter with salt, garlic, parsley, chives, lemon juice and zest in a bowl.
3. Place the lobster in the Ninja Foodi Smart XL grill.
4. Cover the Ninja Foodi Grill's hood and select the Manual settings.
5. Set the temperature to 350 degrees F and cook on the "Grill" Mode for 6 minutes.
6. Pour the butter mixture, black pepper, salt and oil on top, cover and cook for 5 minutes.
7. Garnish with lemon wedges and red pepper flakes.
8. Serve warm.

Serving Suggestion: Serve the lobster tail with mashed cauliflower.

Variation Tip: Add more herbs of your choice to the lobster.

Nutritional Information Per Serving:

Calories 337 | Fat 20g |Sodium 719mg | Carbs 5.1g | Fiber 0.9g | Sugar 1.4g | Protein 37.8g

Chili-Lime Grilled Salmon

Prep Time: 10 minutes.

Cook Time: 8 minutes.

Serves: 4

Ingredients:

- 1 cup sweet chili sauce
- Juice of 2 limes
- 1/4 cup soy sauce
- 4 (6-ounces) salmon fillets
- Green onions, for garnish
- Lime wedges, for serving

Preparation:

1. Mix chili sauce, lime juice, and soy sauce in a bowl.
2. Keep ½ of this marinade aside and add rest to a shallow tray.
3. Add salmon fillets to this marinade, mix well to coat then cover.
4. Refrigerate this salmon for 3 hours.
5. Place the salmon in the Ninja Foodi Smart XL grill.
6. Brush the remaining marinade on top.
7. Cover the Ninja Foodi Grill's hood and select the Manual settings.
8. Set the temperature to 350 degrees F and cook on the "Grill" Mode for 4 minutes per side.
9. Serve warm.

Serving Suggestion: Serve the salmon with fresh greens and mashed cauliflower.

Variation Tip: Add a drizzle of herbs on top.

Nutritional Information Per Serving:

Calories 301 | Fat 5g |Sodium 340mg | Carbs 4.7g | Fiber 1.2g | Sugar 1.3g | Protein 15.3g

Taco Lime Shrimp

Prep Time: 10 minutes.

Cook Time: 6 minutes.

Serves: 2

Ingredients:

- Juice of 2 limes
- 1/4 cup red enchilada sauce
- 2 tablespoons taco seasoning mix
- 2 tablespoons vegetable oil
- 1 teaspoon garlic powder
- 1 lb. medium shrimp, peeled and deveined
- Black pepper, to taste
- Freshly chopped cilantro, for garnish

Preparation:

1. Mix enchilada sauce, taco seasoning, oil, garlic powder, and black pepper in a bowl.
2. Keep ½ of this marinade aside and add rest to a shallow tray.
3. Add shrimp to this marinade, mix well to coat then cover.
4. Refrigerate the shrimp for 15 minutes.
5. Place the shrimp in the Ninja Foodi Smart XL grill.
6. Brush the remaining marinade on top.
7. Cover the Ninja Foodi Grill's hood and select the Manual settings.
8. Set the temperature to 350 degrees F and cook on the "Grill" Mode for 3 minutes per side.
9. Serve warm.

Serving Suggestion: Serve the skewers with kale cucumber salad.

Variation Tip: Add diced onion and bell peppers to the skewers as well.

Nutritional Information Per Serving:

Calories 248 | Fat 23g |Sodium 350mg | Carbs 8g | Fiber 6.3g | Sugar 1g | Protein 40.3g

Grilled Fish Steaks

Prep Time: 15 minutes.

Cook Time: 10 minutes.

Serves: 2

Ingredients:

- 11 garlic cloves, minced
- 6 tablespoons olive oil
- 1 teaspoon dried basil
- 1 teaspoon salt
- 1 teaspoon ground black pepper
- 1 tablespoon lemon juice
- 1 tablespoon chopped fresh parsley
- 2 (6 ounce) fillets halibut

Preparation:

1. Mix parsley, lemon juice, black pepper, salt, basil, oil and garlic in a bowl.
2. Brush this mixture over the halibut fillets, liberally.
3. Cover and marinate the fish for 30 minutes in the refrigerator.
4. Place the halibut in the Ninja Foodi Smart XL grill.
5. Cover the Ninja Foodi Grill's hood and select the Manual settings.
6. Set the temperature to 350 degrees F and cook on the "Grill" Mode for 5 minutes per side.
7. Serve warm.

Serving Suggestion: Serve the steaks with mayo dip.

Variation Tip: Add butter to the fish before serving.

Nutritional Information Per Serving:

Calories 405 | Fat 22.7g |Sodium 227mg | Carbs 6.1g | Fiber 1.4g | Sugar 0.9g | Protein 45.2g

Snack and Side Recipes

Wrapped Stuffed Jalapenos

Prep Time: 20 minutes.

Cook Time: 10 minutes.

Serves: 12

Ingredients:

- 24 jalapeno peppers
- ½ cup sausages, cooked and crumbled
- 2 cups shredded cheddar cheese
- 12 bacon strips, cut in half

Preparation:

1. Cut each jalapeno in half lengthwise and remove the seeds.
2. Stuff the jalapeno halves with sausage, cheese and wrap each with a piece of bacon strip.
3. Secure the wrapped jalapenos with a toothpick.
4. Place the jalapenos in the Ninja Foodi Smart XL grill.
5. Cover the Ninja Foodi Grill's hood and select the Manual settings.
6. Set the temperature to 350 degrees F and cook on the "Grill" Mode for 10 minutes.
7. Serve warm.

Serving Suggestion: Serve the jalapenos with cheese dip.

Variation Tip: Add cream cheese or cream to the filling for a rich texture.

Nutritional Information Per Serving:

Calories 132 | Fat 10g |Sodium 994mg | Carbs 1g | Fiber 0.4g | Sugar 3g | Protein 8g

Mushroom Bacon Bites

Prep Time: 15 minutes.

Cook Time: 16 minutes.

Serves: 12

Ingredients:

- 24 fresh mushrooms
- 12 bacon strips, halved
- 1 cup barbecue sauce

Preparation:

1. Wrap each mushroom with one bacon pieces and secure it with a toothpick.
2. Thread the wrapped mushrooms on a wooden skewer.
3. Brush the wrapped mushrooms with barbecue sauce.
4. Place the mushrooms in the Ninja Foodi Smart XL grill.
5. Cover the Ninja Foodi Grill's hood and select the Manual settings.
6. Set the temperature to 350 degrees F and cook on the "Grill" Mode for 8 minutes per side.
7. Serve warm.

Serving Suggestion: Serve the mushroom bites with Sugar-free BBQ sauce.

Variation Tip: Add piri piri sauce to season bacon for tangy taste.

Nutritional Information Per Serving:

Calories 82 | Fat 6g |Sodium 620mg | Carbs 5g | Fiber 2.4g | Sugar 1.2g | Protein 12g

Grilled Eggplant Parmesan

Prep Time: 10 minutes.

Cook Time: 10 minutes.

Serves: 4

Ingredients:

- 1 (2 lbs.) eggplant, cut into 8 slices
- 1/2 teaspoon salt
- 1 tablespoon olive oil
- 1/2 teaspoon pepper
- 1 log (1 lb.) fresh mozzarella cheese, cut into sixteen slices
- 1 large tomato, cut into eight slices
- 1/2 cup Parmesan cheese, shredded
- Chopped fresh basil or parsley

Preparation:

1. Rub the eggplant slices with black pepper, oil and salt.
2. Place the eggplant in the Ninja Foodi Smart XL grill.
3. Cover the Ninja Foodi Grill's hood and select the Manual settings.
4. Set the temperature to 350 degrees F and cook on the "Grill" Mode for 4 minutes per side.
5. Top each eggplant slice with a tomato slice, 2 mozzarella cheese slices and parmesan cheese on top.
6. Cover and cook for 2 minutes on Bake Mode until the cheese is melted.
7. Garnish with parsley and serve warm.

Serving Suggestion: Serve the eggplant with crispy bacon crumbled on top.

Variation Tip: Add garlic salt on top for more taste.

Nutritional Information Per Serving:

Calories 449 | Fat 31g |Sodium 723mg | Carbs 2g | Fiber 2.5g | Sugar 2g | Protein 26g

Zucchini Cheese Roulades

Prep Time: 10 minutes.

Cook Time: 6 minutes.

Serves: 6

Ingredients:

- 1 cup ricotta cheese
- 1/4 cup Parmesan cheese, grated
- 2 tablespoons fresh basil, minced
- 1 tablespoon capers, drained
- 1 tablespoon Greek olives, chopped
- 1 teaspoon lemon zest, grated
- 1 tablespoon lemon juice
- 1/8 teaspoon salt
- 1/8 teaspoon black pepper
- 4 medium zucchinis, sliced

Preparation:

1. Mix ricotta cheese with the rest of the ingredients except the zucchini slices in a bowl.
2. Place the zucchini slices in the Ninja Foodi Smart XL grill.
3. Cover the Ninja Foodi Grill's hood and select the Manual settings.
4. Set the temperature to 350 degrees F and cook on the "Grill" Mode for 3 minutes per side.
5. Transfer the slices to a working surface and add 1 tablespoon of the ricotta mixture on top at the end of each slice.
6. Roll the zucchini slices and secure them with a toothpick.
7. Serve.

Serving Suggestion: Serve the roulades with fresh greens.

Variation Tip: Add chopped spinach to filling.

Nutritional Information Per Serving:

Calories 24 | Fat 1g |Sodium 236mg | Carbs 2g | Fiber 0.3g | Sugar 0.1g | Protein 1g

Wrapped Shrimp

Prep Time: 10 minutes.

Cook Time: 8 minutes.

Serves: 6

Ingredients:

- 12 jumbo shrimp
- 1/4 cup Italian salad dressing
- 6 bacon strips, cut in half

Preparation:

1. Mix shrimp with Italian salad dressing in a bowl.
2. Wrap each shrimp with a piece of bacon.
3. Thread the wrapped shrimp on wooden skewers.
4. Place the shrimp in the Ninja Foodi Smart XL grill.
5. Cover the Ninja Foodi Grill's hood and select the Manual settings.
6. Set the temperature to 350 degrees F and cook on the "Grill" Mode for 4 minutes per side.
7. Serve warm.

Serving Suggestion: Serve the shrimp with guacamole salad.

Variation Tip: Add a drizzle of taco seasoning.

Nutritional Information Per Serving:

Calories 110 | Fat 6g |Sodium 220mg | Carbs 1g | Fiber 2.4g | Sugar 1.2g | Protein 12g

Bacon Jalapenos

Prep Time: 15 minutes.

Cook Time: 10 minutes.

Serves: 24

Ingredients:

- 1 cup shredded cheddar cheese
- 3 ounces cream cheese, softened
- 24 jalapeno peppers
- 12 bacon strips, halved

Preparation:

1. Cut each jalapeno in half lengthwise and remove the seeds.
2. Mix cream cheese with shredded cheddar cheese in a bowl.
3. Stuff the jalapeno halves with cream cheese mixture and wrap each with a piece of bacon strip.
4. Secure the wrapped jalapenos with a toothpick.
5. Place the jalapenos in the Ninja Foodi Smart XL grill.
6. Cover the Ninja Foodi Grill's hood and select the Manual settings.
7. Set the temperature to 350 degrees F and cook on the "Grill" Mode for 10 minutes.
8. Serve warm.

Serving Suggestion: Serve the jalapenos with roasted broccoli florets.

Variation Tip: Drizzle lemon garlic butter on top before cooking.

Nutritional Information Per Serving:

Calories 56 | Fat 4g | Sodium 634mg | Carbs 1g | Fiber 1.4g | Sugar 1g | Protein 3g

Grilled Zucchini with Chicken

Prep Time: 10 minutes.

Cook Time: 6 minutes.

Serves: 4

Ingredients:

- 2 zucchinis, cut diagonally into slices
- 1/8 teaspoon salt
- 1/8 teaspoon black pepper

TOPPING

- 1/4 cup water
- 3 tablespoons erythritol
- 2 tablespoons soy sauce
- 1 tablespoon creamy peanut butter
- 1 teaspoon lime juice
- 1/4 teaspoon ground ginger
- 1/4 teaspoon cayenne pepper
- 1 cup shredded cooked chicken
- 2 tablespoons red onion, chopped
- Julienned carrot and fresh cilantro, chopped

Preparation:

1. Mix the zucchini slices with black pepper and salt.
2. Place the zucchini slices in the Ninja Foodi Smart XL grill.
3. Cover the Ninja Foodi Grill's hood and select the Manual settings.
4. Set the temperature to 350 degrees F and cook on the "Grill" Mode for 3 minutes per side.
5. Mix and cook the topping ingredients in a saucepan for 3 minutes.
6. Add the toppings mixture over the grilled zucchini slices.
7. Serve warm.

Serving Suggestion: Serve the grilled zucchini with mashed cauliflower.

Variation Tip: Coat the zucchini with crushed pork rinds before grilling.

Nutritional Information Per Serving:

Calories 38 | Fat 7g |Sodium 316mg | Carbs 4g | Fiber 0.3g | Sugar 0.3g | Protein 3g

Grilled Guacamole

Prep Time: 10 minutes.

Cook Time: 4 minutes.

Serves: 6

Ingredients:

- 1 red onion, cut into 1/2-inch slices
- 2 plum tomatoes, halved and seeded
- 1 jalapeno pepper, halved and seeded
- 2 tablespoons canola oil
- 3 ripe avocados, halved and pitted
- 1/4 cup fresh cilantro leaves, chopped
- 2 tablespoons lime juice
- 2 teaspoons ground cumin
- 3/4 teaspoon salt

Preparation:

1. Brush the avocados with oil.
2. Place the avocado in the Ninja Foodi Smart XL grill.
3. Cover the Ninja Foodi Grill's hood and select the Manual settings.
4. Set the temperature to 350 degrees F and cook on the "Grill" Mode for 4 minutes.
5. Mash grilled avocados in a bowl then stir in rest of the ingredients.
6. Mix well and serve.

Serving Suggestion: Serve the guacamole with zucchini chips.

Variation Tip: Add bell peppers or crumbled bacon as well.

Nutritional Information Per Serving:

Calories 85 | Fat 8g |Sodium 146mg | Carbs 5g | Fiber 0.1g | Sugar 0.4g | Protein 1g

Vegetarian Recipes

Grilled Cauliflower with Miso Mayo

Prep Time: 15 minutes.

Cook Time: 17 minutes.

Serves: 4

Ingredients:

- 1 cauliflower head
- 1/2 teaspoon salt
- 4 tablespoons unsalted butter
- 1/4 cup vinegar-based hot sauce
- 1 tablespoon sugar-free ketchup
- 1 tablespoon soy sauce
- 1/2 cup mayonnaise
- 2 tablespoons white miso
- 1 tablespoon lemon juice
- 1/2 teaspoon black pepper
- 2 scallions, sliced

Preparation:

1. Add cauliflower to a large bowl and heat in the microwave to steam for 5 minutes.
2. Mix butter with soy sauce, ketchup, and hot sauce in a small saucepan and cook for 2 minutes.
3. Brush this mixture over the cauliflower.
4. Place the cauliflower in the Ninja Foodi Smart XL grill.
5. Cover the Ninja Foodi Grill's hood and select the Manual settings.
6. Set the temperature to 350 degrees F and cook on the "Grill" Mode for 5 minutes per side.
7. Mix mayo with the rest of the ingredients in a bowl.
8. Serve the cauliflower steaks with mayo sauce.

Serving Suggestion: Serve the cauliflower with lemon wedges.

Variation Tip: Add roasted asparagus on the side.

Nutritional Information Per Serving:

Calories 93 | Fat 3g |Sodium 510mg | Carbs 2g | Fiber 3g | Sugar 4g | Protein 4g

Grilled Asparagus

Prep Time: 15 minutes.

Cook Time: 6 minutes.

Serves: 4

Ingredients:

- 2 lb. asparagus, stalks trimmed
- 2 tablespoons olive oil
- Salt, to taste
- Black pepper, to taste

Preparation:

1. Toss asparagus with oil, black pepper and salt.
2. Place the asparagus in the Ninja Foodi Smart XL grill.
3. Cover the Ninja Foodi Grill's hood and select the Manual settings.
4. Set the temperature to 350 degrees F and cook on the "Grill" Mode for 3 minutes per side.
5. Serve.

Serving Suggestion: Serve the asparagus with fresh herbs on top.

Variation Tip: Add a drizzle of red pepper flakes and parmesan on top.

Nutritional Information Per Serving:

Calories 351 | Fat 19g |Sodium 412mg | Carbs 3g | Fiber 0.3g | Sugar 1g | Protein 23g

Jalapeño Poppers with Smoked Gouda

Prep Time: 15 minutes.

Cook Time: 5 minutes.

Serves: 6

Ingredients:

- 12 large jalapeño chiles
- 4 ounces cream cheese
- 1 cup smoked Gouda, shredded
- Salt, to taste
- Chopped fresh cilantro for serving

Preparation:

1. Cut the jalapenos chiles in half lengthwise and remove the seeds.
2. Mix cream cheese, gouda, and salt in a bowl.
3. Stuff this cheese mixture in the chilies.
4. Place the chiles in the Ninja Foodi Smart XL grill.
5. Cover the Ninja Foodi Grill's hood and select the Manual settings.
6. Set the temperature to 350 degrees F and cook on the "Grill" Mode for 5 minutes.
7. Garnish with cilantro and serve warm.

Serving Suggestion: Serve the poppers with a drizzle of parmesan on top.

Variation Tip: Add shredded chicken to the filling.

Nutritional Information Per Serving:

Calories 136 | Fat 20g |Sodium 249mg | Carbs 4g | Fiber 2g | Sugar 3g | Protein 4g

Grilled Broccoli

Prep Time: 15 minutes.

Cook Time: 18 minutes.

Serves: 4

Ingredients:

- 2 lbs. broccoli
- 1/4 cup olive oil
- 2 tablespoons Worcestershire sauce
- 1 tablespoon soy sauce
- 3 tablespoons sugar-free ketchup
- 1 tablespoon choc-zero maple syrup
- 3 garlic cloves, minced
- 1/2 teaspoon salt
- Black pepper, to taste
- 1/4 teaspoon crushed red pepper flakes
- 1/4 cup Parmesan, grated
- Lemon wedges, for serving

Preparation:

1. Mix oil, sauces, ketchup, choc-zero maple syrup, salt, black pepper and red peppers flakes in a bowl.
2. Toss in broccoli, mix well, cover and marinate for 10 minutes.
3. Place the broccoli in the Ninja Foodi Smart XL grill.
4. Cover the Ninja Foodi Grill's hood and select the Manual settings.
5. Set the temperature to 350 degrees F and cook on the "Grill" Mode for 4 minutes per side.
6. Garnish with Parmesan cheese and lemon wedges.
7. Serve warm.

Serving Suggestion: Serve the broccoli with a drizzle of coconut shred on top.

Variation Tip: Add a drizzle of sesame seeds and oil.

Nutritional Information Per Serving:

Calories 361 | Fat 10g | Sodium 218mg | Carbs 6g | Fiber 10g | Sugar 30g | Protein 14g

Grilled Carrots with Avocado and Mint

Prep Time: 10 minutes.

Cook Time: 8 minutes.

Serves: 4

Ingredients:

- 1 teaspoon cumin seeds
- 3 tablespoons lemon juice
- 2 teaspoons choc-zero maple syrup
- ¼ cup 2 tablespoons olive oil
- 1 serrano chile, seeds removed, sliced
- 1 (1") piece ginger, peeled, grated
- Salt, to taste
- 1½ lb. medium carrots, halved lengthwise
- 2 avocados, peeled and cut into large pieces
- ½ cup mint leaves

Preparation:

1. Crush cumin seeds in a mortar with a pestle.
2. Mix the cumin seeds with lemon juice, choc-zero maple syrup, oil, chile, ginger, and salt in a large bowl.
3. Toss in carrots and mix well to coat.
4. Place the carrots in the Ninja Foodi Smart XL grill.
5. Cover the Ninja Foodi Grill's hood and select the Manual settings.
6. Set the temperature to 350 degrees F and cook on the "Grill" Mode for 4 minutes per side.
7. Serve the carrots with mint leaves and avocados.

Serving Suggestion: Serve the carrots with boiled cauliflower rice.

Variation Tip: Top the carrots with feta cheese before serving.

Nutritional Information Per Serving:

Calories 341 | Fat 24g |Sodium 547mg | Carbs 6.4g | Fiber 1.2g | Sugar 1g | Protein 10.3g

Grilled Cauliflower Wedges with Herb Tarator

Prep Time: 10 minutes.

Cook Time: 6 minutes.

Serves: 2

Ingredients:

Tarator

- ¼ cup toasted almonds, sliced
- 2 garlic cloves, grated
- 1 cup dill, chopped
- ½ cup mint leaves
- ½ cup tahini
- ⅓ cup lemon juice
- Salt and black pepper, to taste

Cauliflower

- 1 small cauliflower, cut into wedges
- ¼ cup olive oil
- ½ teaspoons ground coriander
- ½ teaspoons ground cumin
- ½ teaspoons turmeric
- Handful of tender herbs

Preparation:

1. Blend garlic with 1/3 cup water, tahini, mint, dill, garlic, black pepper, salt and lemon juice in a blender until smooth.
2. Toss cauliflower wedges with oil, turmeric and the rest of the ingredients in a bowl.
3. Place the cauliflower wedges in the Ninja Foodi Smart XL grill.
4. Cover the Ninja Foodi Grill's hood and select the Manual settings.
5. Set the temperature to 350 degrees F and cook on the "Grill" Mode for 3 minutes per side.
6. Mix the tarator sauce with cauliflower wedges in a bowl to coat.
7. Garnish with almonds and herbs.
8. Enjoy.

Serving Suggestion: Serve the cauliflower with butter sauce and bacon on top.

Variation Tip: Add boiled green beans to the cauliflower before serving.

Nutritional Information Per Serving:

Calories 378 | Fat 3.8g |Sodium 620mg | Carbs 3.3g | Fiber 2.4g | Sugar 1.2g | Protein 5.4g

Mushrooms with Béarnaise Yogurt

Prep Time: 15 minutes.

Cook Time: 6 minutes.

Serves: 4

Ingredients:

Yogurt sauce

- 1 shallot, chopped
- 2 sprigs tarragon chopped
- 1/2 teaspoon black peppercorns, crushed
- 1 tablespoon white wine vinegar
- 1 cup Greek yogurt
- 2 tablespoons lemon juice
- 1 tablespoon olive oil
- Salt, to taste

Mushrooms

- 1 tablespoon coriander seeds
- 1 teaspoon salt
- 1 teaspoon mustard powder
- 1 teaspoon paprika
- 12 ounces maitake mushrooms, torn into large pieces
- 2 tablespoons olive oil

Preparation:

1. Blend yogurt with the rest of the sauce ingredients in a blender until smooth.
2. Grind and the rest of the spices for mushrooms in a grinder.
3. Mix the mushrooms with this spice mixture and oil in a bowl.
4. Place the mushrooms in the Ninja Foodi Smart XL grill.
5. Cover the Ninja Foodi Grill's hood and select the Manual settings.
6. Set the temperature to 350 degrees F and cook on the "Grill" Mode for 3 minutes per side.
7. Serve them with yogurt sauce.

Serving Suggestion: Serve the mushrooms with crispy keto bread.

Variation Tip: Add cheese on top of the grilled mushrooms.

Nutritional Information Per Serving:

Calories 391 | Fat 2.2g |Sodium 276mg | Carbs 2.7g | Fiber 0.9g | Sugar 1.4g | Protein 8.8g

Grilled Green Tomatoes

Prep Time: 10 minutes.

Cook Time: 6 minutes.

Serves: 4

Ingredients:

- 3 unripe green tomatoes, sliced
- 1 tablespoon red wine vinegar
- Black pepper, to taste
- 8 ounces mozzarella, torn into pieces
- 1 bunch scallions, sliced
- 1 jalapeno, sliced
- 1/2 cup roasted almonds, chopped
- 1 cup cilantro leaves, chopped
- Flaky sea salt, to taste

Preparation:

1. Rub green tomatoes with black pepper and vinegar.
2. Place the green tomatoes in the Ninja Foodi Smart XL grill.
3. Cover the Ninja Foodi Grill's hood and select the Manual settings.
4. Set the temperature to 350 degrees F and cook on the "Grill" Mode for 3 minutes per side.
5. Serve the grilled green tomatoes with the remaining ingredients on top.
6. Enjoy.

Serving Suggestion: Serve the green tomatoes with mashed cauliflower.

Variation Tip: Add crispy fried onion on top for better taste.

Nutritional Information Per Serving's

Calories 304 | Fat 31g |Sodium 834mg | Carbs 4.4g | Fiber 0.2g | Sugar 0.3g | Protein 4.6g

Grilled Green Beans

Prep Time: 15 minutes.

Cook Time: 7 minutes.

Serves: 4

Ingredients:

- 1 lb. green beans, ends trimmed
- 3 tablespoons olive oil
- 2 tablespoons soy sauce
- 1 tablespoon chili garlic paste
- 2 teaspoons choc-zero maple syrup
- Pinch red pepper flakes
- Salt, to taste
- Sesame seeds, for garnish
- Sliced green onions, for garnish
- Roasted peanuts, chopped

Preparation:

1. Toss green beans with oil, soy sauce, garlic paste, choc-zero maple syrup, salt, and red pepper flakes in a bowl.
2. Place the green beans in the Ninja Foodi Smart XL grill.
3. Cover the Ninja Foodi Grill's hood and select the Manual settings.
4. Set the temperature to 350 degrees F and cook on the "Grill" Mode for 7 minutes.
5. Garnish with green onions, sesame seeds, and peanuts.
6. Serve warm.

Serving Suggestion: Serve the green beans with roasted mushrooms.

Variation Tip: Add lemon zest and lemon juice on top for better taste.

Nutritional Information Per Serving:

Calories 324 | Fat 5g |Sodium 432mg | Carbs 3.1g | Fiber 0.3g | Sugar 1g | Protein 5.7g

Grilled Eggplant with Tahini-Yogurt Sauce

Prep Time: 15 minutes.

Cook Time: 10 minutes.

Serves: 4

Ingredients:

- 2 lbs. small eggplant, sliced
- 2 garlic heads, peeled
- 1 cup Greek yogurt
- 1 tablespoon tahini
- Salt, to taste
- 1 lemon, halved
- Sumac, for serving

Preparation:

1. Blend yogurt with tahini, salt, and garlic in a blender.
2. Place the eggplant slices in the Ninja Foodi Smart XL grill.
3. Cover the Ninja Foodi Grill's hood and select the Manual settings.
4. Set the temperature to 350 degrees F and cook on the "Grill" Mode for 5 minutes per side.
5. Serve the grilled eggplant slices with yogurt on top.
6. Garnish with sumac and lemon halves on top.
7. Enjoy.

Serving Suggestion: Serve the eggplant with zucchini noodles.

Variation Tip: Add green beans around the eggplants before serving.

Nutritional Information Per Serving:

Calories 318 | Fat 15.7g | Sodium 124mg | Carbs 7g | Fiber 0.1g | Sugar 0.3g | Protein 4.9g

Dessert Recipes

Carrot Cake Muffins

Prep Time: 15 minutes.

Cook Time: 20 minutes.

Serves: 6

Ingredients:

- 1 cup almond flour
- 1/2 cup Lakanto monk fruit
- 1 teaspoon baking powder
- 1 teaspoon cinnamon
- 1/2 teaspoon salt
- 3/4 cup olive oil
- 2 eggs, beaten
- 3 small carrots, shredded

Preparation:

1. Mix all the muffin ingredients except carrot, in a bowl until smooth.
2. Fold in carrot and divide this muffin batter in a greased muffin tray.
3. Place the muffin tray in the Ninja Foodi Smart XL grill.
4. Cover the Ninja Foodi Grill's hood and select the Manual settings.
5. Set the temperature to 350 degrees F and cook on the "Bake" Mode for 20 minutes.
6. Serve.

Serving Suggestion: Serve the muffins with chocolate syrup on top.

Variation Tip: Add crushed cashews to the muffins.

Nutritional Information Per Serving:

Calories 153 | Fat 1g |Sodium 8mg | Carbs 6.6g | Fiber 0.8g | Sugar 56g | Protein 1g

Zucchini Muffins

Prep Time: 15 minutes.

Cook Time: 20 minutes.

Serves: 6

Ingredients:

- 2 cups shredded zucchini
- 2/3 cup coconut flour
- 1/2 cup swerve sweetener
- 1/4 cup unflavored whey protein powder
- 2 teaspoons baking powder
- 1 teaspoon cinnamon
- 1/2 teaspoon ginger
- 1/4 teaspoon salt
- 1/8 teaspoons cloves
- 6 large eggs
- 1/4 cup butter, melted
- 3 to 4 tablespoons water
- 1/2 cup walnuts, chopped

Preparation:

1. Mix all the muffin ingredients except walnuts and zucchini, in a bowl until smooth.
2. Fold in walnuts and zucchini and mix evenly.
3. Divide this muffin batter in a greased muffin tray.
4. Place the muffin tray in the Ninja Foodi Smart XL grill.
5. Cover the Ninja Foodi Grill's hood and select the Manual settings.
6. Set the temperature to 350 degrees F and cook on the "Bake" Mode for 20 minutes.
7. Serve.

Serving Suggestion: Serve the muffins with creamy frosting on top.

Variation Tip: Add crushed pecans to the muffins.

Nutritional Information Per Serving:

Calories 195 | Fat 3g |Sodium 355mg | Carbs 7.7g | Fiber 1g | Sugar 25g | Protein 1g

Double Chocolate Muffins

Prep Time: 15 minutes.

Cook Time: 20 minutes.

Serves: 6

Ingredients:

- 1/2 cup coconut flour
- 3/4 teaspoons baking soda
- 2 tablespoons cocoa powder
- 1/2 teaspoon salt, to taste
- 1 teaspoon cinnamon
- 1/2 teaspoon nutmeg
- 3 large eggs
- 2/3 cup granular sweetener
- 2 teaspoons vanilla extract
- 1 tablespoon oil
- 1 cup zucchini, grated
- 1/4 cup heavy cream
- 1/3 cup sugar-free chocolate chips

Preparation:

1.   Mix all the muffin ingredients except zucchini and chocolate chips in a bowl until smooth.
2.   Fold in zucchini and chocolate chips, then mix evenly.
3.   Now divide this muffin batter into a greased muffin tray.
4.   Place the muffin tray in the Ninja Foodi Smart XL grill.
5.   Cover the Ninja Foodi Grill's hood and select the Manual settings.
6.   Set the temperature to 350 degrees F and cook on the "Bake" Mode for 20 minutes.
7.   Serve.

Serving Suggestion: Serve the muffins with whipped cream on top.

Variation Tip: Add crushed walnuts or pecans to the muffins.

Nutritional Information Per Serving:

Calories 203 | Fat 8.9g |Sodium 340mg | Carbs 7.2g | Fiber 1.2g | Sugar 11.3g | Protein 5.3g

Blueberry Muffins

Prep Time: 15 minutes.

Cook Time: 20 minutes.

Serves: 6

Ingredients:

- 2 ½ cup blanched almond flour
- ½ cup erythritol
- 1 ½ teaspoons baking powder
- ¼ teaspoons sea salt
- 1/3 cup coconut oil
- 1/3 cup unsweetened almond milk
- 3 large eggs
- ½ teaspoons vanilla extract
- 3/4 cup blueberries

Preparation:

1. Mix all the muffin ingredients except berries, in a bowl until smooth.
2. Fold in blueberries and divide this muffin batter in a greased muffin tray.
3. Place the muffin tray in the Ninja Foodi Smart XL grill.
4. Cover the Ninja Foodi Grill's hood and select the Manual settings.
5. Set the temperature to 350 degrees F and cook on the "Bake" Mode for 20 minutes.
6. Serve.

Serving Suggestion: Serve the muffin with keto blueberry sauce on top.

Variation Tip: Add chopped nuts to the muffins.

Nutritional Information Per Serving:

Calories 248 | Fat 16g |Sodium 95mg | Carbs 8.4g | Fiber 0.3g | Sugar 10g | Protein 14.1g

Chocolate Chip Muffins

Prep Time: 15 minutes.

Cook Time: 20 minutes.

Serves: 6

Ingredients:

- 2 1/2 cups almond flour
- 1/4 teaspoon salt
- 2 teaspoons baking powder
- 1/2 cup granulated erythritol
- 1/3 cup butter melted
- 3 large eggs
- 6 tablespoons almond milk
- 1 teaspoon vanilla extract
- 1/2 cup sugar-free chocolate chips

Preparation:

1. Mix all the muffin ingredients except chocolate chips, in a bowl until smooth.
2. Fold in chocolate chips and divide this muffin batter in a greased muffin tray.
3. Place the muffin tray in the Ninja Foodi Smart XL grill.
4. Cover the Ninja Foodi Grill's hood and select the Manual settings.
5. Set the temperature to 350 degrees F and cook on the "Bake" Mode for 20 minutes.
6. Serve.

Serving Suggestion: Serve the muffins with keto chocolate syrup on top.

Variation Tip: Add crushed walnuts or pecans to the muffins.

Nutritional Information Per Serving:

Calories 198 | Fat 14g |Sodium 272mg | Carbs 7g | Fiber 1g | Sugar 9.3g | Protein 1.3g

Chocolate Mini Tarts

Prep Time: 15 minutes.

Cook Time: 20 minutes.

Serves: 6

Ingredients:

Crust

- 1 ¼ cups almond flour
- 2 tablespoons powdered erythritol
- ¼ cup butter

Chocolate filling

- ½ cup unsweetened dark chocolate chips
- ½ cup heavy cream
- 1 teaspoon butter
- 3 tablespoons powdered erythritol

Preparation:

1. Blend almond flour with erythritol and butter in a food processor.
2. Divide this crust mixture into a greased mini muffin tray.
3. Place the muffin tray in the Ninja Foodi Smart XL grill.
4. Cover the Ninja Foodi Grill's hood and select the Manual settings.
5. Set the temperature to 350 degrees F and cook on the "Bake" Mode for 20 minutes.
6. Blend melted chocolate with cream, butter and erythritol in a bowl.
7. Divide this mixture into the baked crust.
8. Allow the filling to cool then refrigerate for 30 minutes.
9. Serve.

Serving Suggestion: Serve the tarts with chocolate sauce and cacao nibs on top.

Variation Tip: Add crushed walnuts or pecans to the filling.

Nutritional Information Per Serving:

Calories 217 | Fat 12g |Sodium 79mg | Carbs 8g | Fiber 1.1g | Sugar 18g | Protein 5g

Blueberry Mini Tarts

Prep Time: 15 minutes.

Cook Time: 30 minutes.

Serves: 6

Ingredients:

Crust

- 1 ¼ cups almond flour
- 2 tablespoons powdered erythritol
- ¼ cup butter

Blueberry filling

- 1 cup blueberries
- 2 tablespoons swerve
- 1 teaspoon lemon juice

Preparation:

1. Blend almond flour with erythritol, and butter in a food processor.
2. Divide this crust mixture into a greased mini muffin tray.
3. Place the muffin tray in the Ninja Foodi Smart XL grill.
4. Cover the Ninja Foodi Grill's hood and select the Manual settings.
5. Set the temperature to 350 degrees F and cook on the "Bake" Mode for 20 minutes.
6. Mix blueberries with swerve and lemon juice in a saucepan.
7. Cook this mixture for 5-10 minutes until soft.
8. Divide this mixture into the baked crust.
9. Allow the filling to cool, then refrigerate for 30 minutes.
1. Serve.

Serving Suggestion: Serve the tarts with fresh blueberries on top.

Variation Tip: Add crushed chocolate on top of the tarts.

Nutritional Information Per Serving:

Calories 245 | Fat 14g |Sodium 122mg | Carbs 8g | Fiber 1.2g | Sugar 12g | Protein 4.3g

Strawberry Mini Tarts

Prep Time: 15 minutes.

Cook Time: 20 minutes.

Serves: 6

Ingredients:

Crust

- 1 ¼ cups Almond flour
- 2 tablespoons powdered erythritol
- ¼ cup butter

Strawberry filling

- 1/2 cup strawberries
- 1 cup cream cheese
- 2 tablespoons swerve

Preparation:

1. Blend almond flour with erythritol, and butter in a food processor.
2. Divide this crust mixture in a greased mini muffin tray.
3. Place the muffin tray in the Ninja Foodi Smart XL grill.
4. Cover the Ninja Foodi Grill's hood and select the Manual settings.
5. Set the temperature to 350 degrees F and cook on the "Bake" Mode for 20 minutes.
6. Blender strawberries with cream cheese and swerve in a blender.
7. Divide this mixture in the baked crust.
8. Allow the filling to cool then refrigerate for 30 minutes.
9. Serve.

Serving Suggestion: Serve the tarts with sliced strawberries on top.

Variation Tip: Add crushed chocolate on top of the tarts.

Nutritional Information Per Serving:

Calories 159 | Fat 3g |Sodium 277mg | Carbs 9g | Fiber 1g | Sugar 9g | Protein 2g

Cinnamon Sugar Muffins

Prep Time: 15 minutes.

Cook Time: 20 minutes.

Serves: 6

Ingredients:

- ½ cup erythritol sweetener
- 5 tablespoons butter, softened
- 1 teaspoon vanilla
- 2 eggs
- ½ cup half and half
- 1 ½ cups almond flour
- 1 tablespoon ground flaxseed
- 2 teaspoons baking powder
- 1 teaspoon cinnamon
- ½ teaspoon ginger
- ½ teaspoon nutmeg

Cinnamon Sugar

- 4 tablespoons butter, melted
- ½ cup granulated erythritol
- 2 teaspoons cinnamon

Preparation:

1. Mix all the muffin ingredients in a bowl until smooth.
2. Divide this muffin batter in a greased muffin tray.
3. Place the muffin tray in the Ninja Foodi Smart XL grill.
4. Cover the Ninja Foodi Grill's hood and select the Manual settings.
5. Set the temperature to 350 degrees F and cook on the "Bake" Mode for 20 minutes.
6. Mix cinnamon with butter and sweetener in a bowl and drizzle over the muffins.
7. Serve.

Serving Suggestion: Serve the muffins with melted chocolate on top.

Variation Tip: Add crushed nuts to the muffins.

Nutritional Information Per Serving:

Calories 118 | Fat 20g |Sodium 192mg | Carbs 6.8g | Fiber 0.9g | Sugar 19g | Protein 5.2g

30-Day Meal Plan

Week 1

Day 1:

Breakfast: Bacon on The Grill

Lunch: Garlicky Lemongrass Chicken

Snack: Wrapped Stuffed Jalapenos

Dinner: Grilled Cauliflower with Miso Mayo

Dessert: Cinnamon Sugar Muffins

Day 2:

Breakfast: Grilled Ham

Lunch: Grilled Chicken Breasts with Lemon

Snack: Grilled Guacamole

Dinner: Grilled Cauliflower Wedges with Herb Tarator

Dessert: Blueberry Muffins

Day 3:

Breakfast: Grilled Fried Eggs

Lunch: Big Bob Gibson's Chicken

Snack: Zucchini Cheese Roulades

Dinner: Grilled Green Tomatoes

Dessert: Chocolate Mini Tarts

Day 4:

Breakfast: Cheesy Eggs

Lunch: Baja-Style Rosemary Chicken Skewers

Snack: Grilled Zucchini with Chicken

Dinner: Grilled Carrots with Avocado and Mint

Dessert: Zucchini Muffins

Day 5:

Breakfast: Grilled Sausages

Lunch: Piri Piri Chicken

Snack: Bacon Jalapenos

Dinner: Grilled Eggplant with Tahini-Yogurt Sauce

Dessert: Double Chocolate Muffins

Day 6:

Breakfast: Grilled Breakfast Sausage

Lunch: Grilled Chicken Thighs

Snack: Grilled Eggplant Parmesan

Dinner: Mushrooms with Béarnaise Yogurt

Dessert: Carrot Cake Muffins

Day 7:

Breakfast: Avocado Eggs

Lunch: Grilled Chicken with Chimichurri

Snack: Wrapped Shrimp

Dinner: Grilled Green Beans

Dessert: Chocolate Chip Muffins

Week 2

Day 1:

Breakfast: Grilled Eggs with Prosciutto and Parmesan

Lunch: Grilled Chicken with Mustard Sauce

Snack: Mushroom Bacon Bites

Dinner: Jalapeño Poppers with Smoked Gouda

Dessert: Strawberry Mini Tarts

Day 2:

Breakfast: Grilled Ham

Lunch: Grilled Red Curry Chicken

Snack: Grilled Guacamole

Dinner: Grilled Asparagus

Dessert: Blueberry Muffins

Day 3:

Breakfast: Grilled Fried Eggs

Lunch: Grilled Chicken and Radishes

Snack: Zucchini Cheese Roulades

Dinner: Grilled Broccoli

Dessert: Chocolate Mini Tarts

Day 4:

Breakfast: Cheesy Eggs

Lunch: Grilled Chicken with Olives

Snack: Grilled Zucchini with Chicken

Dinner: Grilled Fish Steaks

Dessert: Zucchini Muffins

Day 5:

Breakfast: Grilled Sausages

Lunch: Tamarind-Glazed Chicken Wings

Snack: Bacon Jalapenos

Dinner: Lemon Salmon Skewers

Dessert: Double Chocolate Muffins

Day 6:

Breakfast: Grilled Breakfast Sausage

Lunch: Coconut and Lemongrass Steak Skewers

Snack: Grilled Eggplant Parmesan

Dinner: Hot Shot Salmon

Dessert: Carrot Cake Muffins

Day 7:

Breakfast: Avocado Eggs

Lunch: Hasselback Short Rib Bulgogi

Snack: Wrapped Shrimp

Dinner: Chili-Lime Grilled Salmon

Dessert: Chocolate Chip Muffins

Week 3

Day 1:

Breakfast: Bacon on The Grill

Lunch: Lacquered Rib Eye

Snack: Wrapped Stuffed Jalapenos

Dinner: Taco Lime Shrimp

Dessert: Cinnamon Sugar Muffins

Day 2:

Breakfast: Grilled Ham

Lunch: Skirt Steak with Ba Sauce

Snack: Grilled Guacamole

Dinner: Cilantro Lime Grilled Salmon

Dessert: Blueberry Muffins

Day 3:

Breakfast: Grilled Fried Eggs

Lunch: Tri-Tip Steak with Tiger Bite Sauce

Snack: Zucchini Cheese Roulades

Dinner: Grilled Lobster Tail

Dessert: Chocolate Mini Tarts

Day 4:

Breakfast: Cheesy Eggs

Lunch: Soy Sauce–Marinated Grilled Flank Steak

Snack: Grilled Zucchini with Chicken

Dinner: Grilled Tilapia with Tomatoes

Dessert: Zucchini Muffins

Day 5:

Breakfast: Grilled Sausages

Lunch: Grilled Brisket with Scallion-Peanut Salsa

Snack: Bacon Jalapenos

Dinner: Lemony Grilled Salmon

Dessert: Double Chocolate Muffins

Day 6:

Breakfast: Grilled Breakfast Sausage

Lunch: Grilled Rib Eye with Shishito Pepper Salsa

Snack: Grilled Eggplant Parmesan

Dinner: Grilled Halibut with Avocado Salsa

Dessert: Carrot Cake Muffins

Day 7:

Breakfast: Avocado Eggs

Lunch: Grilled Bone-In Rib Eye

Snack: Wrapped Shrimp

Dinner: Spicy Grilled Fish

Dessert: Chocolate Chip Muffins

Week 4

Day 1:

Breakfast: Grilled Eggs with Prosciutto and Parmesan

Lunch: Flank Steak with Zucchini Salsa

Snack: Mushroom Bacon Bites

Dinner: Spicy Grilled Fish

Dessert: Strawberry Mini Tarts

Day 2:

Breakfast: Grilled Ham

Lunch: Coconut-Marinated Short Rib Kebabs

Snack: Grilled Guacamole

Dinner: Spicy Grilled Shrimp

Dessert: Blueberry Muffins

Day 3:

Breakfast: Grilled Fried Eggs

Lunch: Grilled Beef with Broccoli

Snack: Zucchini Cheese Roulades

Dinner: Grilled Chicken Thighs

Dessert: Chocolate Mini Tarts

Day 4:

Breakfast: Cheesy Eggs

Lunch: Hawaiian Rib-Eye Steak

Snack: Grilled Zucchini with Chicken

Dinner: Grilled Chicken with Chimichurri

Dessert: Zucchini Muffins

Day 5:

Breakfast: Grilled Sausages

Lunch: Jalapeño-Marinated Pork Chops

Snack: Bacon Jalapenos

Dinner: Grilled Chicken with Olives

Dessert: Double Chocolate Muffins

Day 6:

Breakfast: Grilled Breakfast Sausage

Lunch: Pork Chops with Radishes

Snack: Grilled Eggplant Parmesan

Dinner: Mushrooms with Béarnaise Yogurt

Dessert: Carrot Cake Muffins

Day 7:

Breakfast: Avocado Eggs

Lunch: Grilled Pork Ribs with Gochujang Sauce

Snack: Wrapped Shrimp

Dinner: Grilled Eggplant with Tahini-Yogurt Sauce

Dessert: Chocolate Chip Muffins

Conclusion

Did you like those low-carb Ninja Foodi XL Grill recipes? Aren't they seem fun and easy enough to cook at home? Well, now is the time to make it all happen and enjoy a delicious low-carb meal to optimize good health. The collection of 80 recipes in this cookbook, along with the 30-day meal plan, will definitely help you get started with the diet and this cooking appliance. The Ninja foodi XL grill has no parallel when it comes to cooking style. It comes with a base unit with a hood and a front control panel. This control panel have one-touch keys to control all the functions and the manual settings. The keys for cooking modes are given at the bottom of the control panel above these keys; you can see an LED display that shows the cooking temperature and time. On both sides of the display, there are keys to increase or decrease that time and temperature. There are a different set of accessories that comes with the Ninja foodi XL grill. And you can use any of these accessories to cook according to the recipe. The grill pan is used for grilling all type of food.

It's about time that you take some actions and set up your ninja food XL grill and start cooking your favorite low carb meal from this cookbook, then share with all your loved ones

CPSIA information can be obtained
at www.ICGtesting.com
Printed in the USA
LVHW062320180721
693060LV00002B/157

9 781801 219013